FINDING YOUR
SOUL
MATE
WITH
THETAHEALING®

FINDING YOUR SOUL MATE

WITH THETAHEALING®

VIANNA STIBAL

Compiled by Guy Stibal from the dictation of Vianna Stibal

HAY HOUSE

Carlsbad, California • New York City
London • Sydney • New Delhi

Published in the United States by: Hay House, Inc.: www.hayhouse.com®
Published in Australia by: Hay House Australia Pty. Ltd.: www.hayhouse.com.au
Published in the United Kingdom by: Hay House UK, Ltd.: www.hayhouse.co.uk
Published in India by: Hay House Publishers India: www.hayhouse.co.in

Cover and interior design: Leanne Siu Anastasi

Interior images: 1, 91, 173 Thinkstockphotos/PongsakornJun; 203 Vianna Stibal;
All other images Shutterstock/PHOTOCREO Michal Bednarek and Shutterstock/
sakkmesterke

Library of Congress Control Number: 2016952574

Tradepaper ISBN: 978-1-4019-5343-0

1st edition, November 2016

Printed in the United States of America

CONTENTS

PART III: LIVING WITH A SOUL MATE

LIST OF EXERCISES

FOREWORD

This book is designed for spiritually romantic people who have not lost faith – faith that somewhere out in the world, a person of like mind is gazing up at the same heavens, a person who could be that special someone. Someone who could share a passion that is divine in nature, creating or recreating a relationship that is felt even unto the soul, reborn with such an intensity that both feel they could be parts of one being. In short, it is for people who are looking for a soul mate.

To me, the basis of this is the mystical, romantic quality of the human spirit that is intrinsic in some of us. It is a natural thing for us to want to be with someone who has a divine understanding of us and to believe that two people can be brought together to fulfill a divine plan, with destiny working toward a higher purpose.

The desire for a soul mate is exactly that: the ancient need to become the divine couple whose union breathes new life into the world on levels beyond the physical.

Seen from this context, finding your soul mate has deeper ramifications. The union of soul mates is about the creation of an energy that is extraordinary. This energy is what some call the philosopher's stone and the Welsh call the Awen – divine inspiration that rises from the passion that rests deep inside us, waiting for the fulfillment that can only be brought by the union of two compatible souls. This inspiration then flows outward to all the other aspects that constitute our existence.

Like a pebble cast into a pool of still water, this union of two souls sends ripples outward in an expression of divine timing on a grand scale. This divine timing works on more than one level. First, the union between two souls stimulates the evolution of the eternal spirits of both people involved. Secondly (and perhaps more importantly), it is designed by the cosmos to inspire others and help them in their spiritual growth. It creates an energy composed of light – one more candle to bring illumination to the world.

Many of us are born into this world knowing what being loved by another person should be like but not knowing how to fulfill this desire in the highest and best way. In order to realize this heart's desire and find ourselves comfortable with another person, we must first love ourselves enough and then we must take a leap of faith. For this is not as easy as it seems. It takes real courage to love someone so completely. Many people know on an instinctual level that feelings for another person that are so intense, so all-encompassing, are risky, and many avoid this kind of close relationship out of pure fear. Some avoid it to the extent that they don't believe in it at all.

Certainly there was a time when I had given up on true love and didn't believe I would find the high priestess that the universe kept telling me was coming. I was even thinking of becoming a monk of some kind and disappearing into asceticism. But on April 1, 1997 (my 37th birthday), as the Hale–Bopp comet passed perihelion, I knew that change was in the air. Like a rainstorm that you can feel on a clear and windless day, something was coming. The rainstorm began in August, and the winds and the waters called Vianna swept me up in a vision of ThetaHealing® that began with one kiss. By the fall of that year we were in love, our destinies merging, and we were on the wings of a prayer.

I believe that soul-mate magnetism is what happened between Vianna and me with that first kiss, and it continues to this day. This book is dedicated to our love story and to all the romantics out there. Now, my friend, go on a journey with Vianna and reaffirm your belief in true love.

Guy Stibal

INTRODUCTION

This book was inspired by my true-life love story with my husband, Guy Stibal. That story started 10 years before I actually met him, when I began to have visions of a man from Montana. At the time, I knew that something was missing from my life – a great and deep love that I felt I had experienced before and would again. I knew that this love was passionate and deep beyond my human understanding. I also felt that once I met this man, we would know each other.

I felt guilty about these visions because I was in a relationship at the time, but they wouldn't go away. They lasted for many years and peaked when I started to do readings and subsequently learned how to manifest. That was when I learned a very important thing: if you don't follow your dreams, you permit others to run your life for you. Until I learned to manifest what I wanted, I lived my life according to what others wanted me to do.

In my relationships before I met Guy, I didn't know how to let myself be loved. I think that this was because I didn't love myself. The relationships didn't work out because of compatibility issues, and I was smart enough to leave them, but I also had the belief that I *had* to leave them before I could find my man from Montana.

Then I came to a point where I found my self-worth and manifested the man whom I wanted. Finally I'd found someone I could envision myself being with for the rest of my life. When I got together with Guy, I could actually see myself sitting on a rocking chair and growing old with him. The missing piece of the puzzle had finally fallen into place. In fact we wrote a book about it together called *On the Wings of Prayer*.

What helped me to manifest a soul mate were the readings and consultations that I did. Through these consultations I found that others were looking for their soul mate as well. In fact, the most frequently asked question about relationships was: 'Will I ever find my soul mate?'

It was only after I got together with Guy that I began to reflect on how to empower people to find that special person. I began by encouraging them to manifest their most compatible soul mate. Then I decided to put our love story into a book to help people see that it was possible to find your soul mate.

As time went on, I could see that while manifesting was effective for some people, by itself it didn't work for everyone. As I did many more readings and encountered thousands of different scenarios, common patterns began to become apparent. As I took ThetaHealing further and developed the belief work, I found that there were many negative belief systems relating to relationships and love. One of the most basic was: 'It is impossible to find a compatible soul mate.'

In this book I will show you how to change these beliefs, find a soul mate, and enjoy a loving relationship with them.

HOW TO USE THIS BOOK

This book is the companion to my first book, *ThetaHealing*, and second book, *Advanced ThetaHealing*. In *ThetaHealing*, I explain the step-by-step processes of the ThetaHealing reading, healing, belief work, feeling work, digging and gene work, and provide an introduction to the planes of existence and additional knowledge for the beginner. *Advanced ThetaHealing* gives an in-depth guide to belief, feeling and digging work, and insights into the planes of existence and the beliefs that I believe are essential for spiritual evolution. It does not include the step-by-step processes of *ThetaHealing*. It is necessary to reach an understanding of these processes in order to fully utilize this current book. However, there is a short description of them in the first chapter.

These techniques are processes of meditation that I believe create physical, psychological, and spiritual healing using the theta brainwave. While in a pure and divine theta state of mind, we are able to connect to the Creator of All That Is through focused prayer. The Creator has given us the fascinating knowledge that you are about to receive. It has changed my life and the lives of many others.

There is, however, one requirement that is absolute with this technique: you must have a central belief in a Creator, God, the

Creator of All That Is, or whatever name you choose. (ThetaHealing has no religious affiliation and I realize that the Creator has many names, including God, Buddha, Nirvana, Allah, Shiva, Goddess, Jesus, Source, and Yahweh.) Then, with study and practice, anyone can do it – anyone who believes in the All That Is essence that flows through all things! The processes of ThetaHealing are not specific to any age, sex, race, color, or creed. Anyone with a pure belief in God can access and use the branches of the ThetaHealing tree.

Even though I am sharing this information with you, I do not accept any responsibility for the changes that may arise from its use. The responsibility is yours – the responsibility you assume when you realize that you have the power to change your life as well as the lives of others.

What I will be attempting to do is to give you some practical spiritual guidance relating to love, relationships, and, particularly, soul mates. You may be looking for love – a love that is divine. You may never have fallen in love before and be looking for that special someone to be with. You may be lonely. There are many lonely people in the world, and it is my hope that this book will assist them to companionship. It gives you pointers not only on how to find a soul mate, but how to keep them as well. And if you already have your soul mate, it will help your relationship with them.

One last important thing before you use this guide. This is a guide for dating and marriage. It is not a license to leave your lover or your present relationship. It has not been designed as a 'relationship destroyer.' Kindly do not include ThetaHealing in a blame game because you want to leave your lover, wife, or husband! You never know, people can change, and underneath all those old outworn beliefs they might just be your compatible or even divine soul mate.

I believe that since the year 1998 more soul mates have been finding each another than at any other time in history. I believe that this is because of the change in the electromagnetic energy of the Earth and the spiritual evolution we are experiencing. This is a time when we are beginning to love ourselves enough to feel deserving of a compatible or even a divine soul mate. I hope that you find yours.

Part I

THE PRINCIPLES OF SOUL MATES

Chapter 1

LOVE AND
THE THETA TECHNIQUE

I believe that there is a special person out there for all of us. Open your eyes to the world around you and you will find them. ThetaHealing can help you. Here's how.

A QUICK REMINDER OF THE THETA TECHNIQUE

In this book you will utilize a technique that takes you into a theta brainwave. In order for you to understand this, I am offering this short summary from my first two books. It is important that you have at least an overview of the branches of the ThetaHealing tree.

The Theta Brainwave

Everything that we do and say is regulated by the frequency of our brainwaves. There are five different brainwaves: alpha, beta, delta, gamma, and theta. The brain is consistently producing waves in all of these frequencies.

A theta brainwave state is a very deep state of relaxation, a dream state, always creative, inspirational, and characterized by very spiritual sensations. I believe this state allows access to the subconscious mind and opens a direct conduit to communication with the divine. I believe that once you say the word 'God,' you are holding a conscious theta wave.

When we are in a theta state of mind, we can send our consciousness beyond this mortal body to what we call the Seventh Plane of Existence to connect with the 'All That Is' energy that is inherent in everything throughout the universe. Studies have shown that healers and the people being healed are both dropping into a theta–delta frequency. This may explain the visionary experiences of some healers.

The way that we reach the All That Is energy is with the following meditation. This mental 'road-map' opens your mind to allow you to reach the Seventh Plane of Existence and stimulates neurons in your brain to connect you to the energy of creation. You go on an internal journey to find the Creator-Self that is inside you and travel outward to the Cosmic Consciousness at the same time.

Go Up to the Seventh Plane

Center yourself in your heart and visualize going down to the Earth. Imagine energy coming up through the bottom of your feet from the center of the Earth and going up out of the top of your head as a beautiful ball of light. You are in this ball of light. Take time to notice what color it is.

Now imagine going up above the universe.

Now imagine going into the light above the universe. It is a beautiful big light.

Imagine going up through that light and you will see another bright light, and another, and another. In fact there are many bright lights. Keep going. Between the lights there is a little bit of dark light, but this is just a layer before the next light, so keep going. You are going up through all the planes of existence.

Finally, you will see a great big bright light. Go through it. As you do so, you are going to see a darker energy, a jelly-like substance. It has all the colors of the rainbow in it. When you go into it, you will see that it changes color. You will see all kinds of shapes and colors. These are the Laws that govern the universe.

In the distance there is a white iridescent light. It is a bluish-white color, like a pearl. Head for this light. Avoid getting distracted by the deep blue light that you will see. This is the Law of Magnetism. It will talk to you and you will have a lovely time, but you can commune with it for hours. If you wish, talk to it after you have gone to the Seventh Plane.

As you get closer to the white light, you may see a pink mist. Keep going until you do see it. This is the Law of Compassion, and it will push you into the special place you're heading for.

There is just energy on the Seventh Plane, not people or things. So, if you see people, go higher.

It is from the Seventh Plane that the Creator of All That Is can perform instant healings and that you can create in every aspect of your life.

Practice going the Seventh Plane of Existence to find the purest essence of the All That Is energy. This process will unlock doors in your mind to connect you with All That Is.

The Reading

Now that you have the background information regarding this technique, we will put all the pieces together for remote viewing, or what I call 'the reading.'

The structure of the reading is simple:

THE READING MEDITATION

1. Center yourself in your heart and send your energy down to Mother Earth.

2. Bring energy back up through your body, opening and aligning all your chakras, all the energy centers of your body, as you go.

3. Go up and out of your crown chakra in a beautiful ball of light. Go out to the universe.

4. Go up through all the planes of existence using the road-map to All That Is (above).

5. Make the connection to the Seventh Plane of Existence and the Creator of All That Is.

6. Make the command and request (the command is to your subconscious, the request is to the Creator) to witness the reading by saying silently:

*'Creator of All That Is, a reading is
commanded for [person's name].'*

7. Go into the person's space and witness whatever you need to for this reading.

8. Once you have finished, rinse yourself off with Seventh-Plane energy and stay connected to it.

Once you are able to do this meditation, you are ready to do belief work. Belief work is important in that it will show you what you believe about relationships and finding a life partner. One of the best ways to find out if you are ready for a soul mate is with ThetaHealing belief and feeling work.

Belief and Feeling Work

Belief work gives us a way of finding out how we really feel about relationships and, just as important, about ourselves. If we are comfortable with ourselves, we can live with ourselves. This means that someone else can live with us, too. If there are inconsistencies within us, however, they will be manifested in the people who are drawn to us. These people will have our negative aspects as well as the positive.

Usually we are not aware of this process, or even of the beliefs we hold. Many of us have had difficult relationships in the past that could have been avoided if we had only had the right psychological and spiritual tools.

There are many conflicting belief systems in relation to matters of the heart. An example would be the person who wants to be completely independent *and at the same time* asks for a soul mate to share their life. These two belief systems obviously conflict with each other.

In reading sessions, I listen to women all the time who say, 'There's nothing out there but rotten men.' As a consequence, all they ever find are rotten men. I hear the same thing from the men I talk with. They say, 'There's nothing out there but women who use men.' Because this is what they believe, that is all they find, since this is what their subconscious believes they want.

Belief work can be easily interpreted and understood from a psychological viewpoint as opening a portal to the subconscious mind to create change within it. Through observing people in belief work sessions, it seems that there is a bubble of protection around the subconscious mind – at least in some people. This protection is created so that the hard-drive of the subconscious can insulate us from pain, or what it perceives might be painful to us, should we attempt to change what ThetaHealing now calls 'programs.'

Programs

Our brain works like a biological super-computer, assessing the information that comes to us and responding to it. How we respond to an experience depends on the information that is given to the subconscious and how it is received and interpreted. When a belief has been accepted as real by the mind, we believe it becomes a 'belief program.'

Programs can work to our benefit or detriment, depending on what they are and how we react to them. Many people, for example, live most of their lives with the hidden program that they cannot succeed. Even if they are very successful for many years, they may suddenly lose everything they own as a result of this program. Without realizing that they are sabotaging themselves, they continue the process. They don't understand that there are programs deep within them, floating in the subconscious mind, waiting for the opportunity to be expressed in the outer world.

Belief work empowers us with the ability to remove these negative programs and replace them with positive ones. This comes about through the perception that we can create change through the most powerful force in the universe: the energy of subatomic particles.

Throughout our lifetime, as we learn and grow, many of us find that change and growth can be difficult. When we are children, our experiences with change can teach us that it can be painful, even dangerous. For instance, it can be traumatic to change schools. If our parents get divorced or a family member or friend dies, the bubble begins to form around our subconscious as a means to insulate us from pain. As we grow older, change and growth (as perceived by the Western mindset) are also in large part perceived as painful. When we lose or change jobs, lose a lover, or as our bodies age, our perceptions of change can become progressively more negative. So, even an attempt for positive change can be seen as painful and the bubble of protection stays in place. As we grow older, it becomes more and more difficult to make changes that might be painful for us. The layers of protection become thicker and thicker.

Belief work is a means to pierce through the layers to the subconscious mind to make change without creating or recreating the pain.

The Belief Levels

We believe that there are four levels of belief within a person where belief programs are held:

1. *The core-belief level:* Core beliefs are what we have been taught and have accepted from childhood in this life. They have become a part of us. They are held as energy in the frontal lobe of the brain.

2. *The genetic level:* On this level, programs are carried over from our ancestors or are added to our genes in this life. These beliefs are stored as energy in the morphogenetic field around the physical DNA. This field of knowledge is what tells the mechanics of the DNA what to do.

3. *The history level:* This level concerns memories from a past life, or deep genetic memories, or collective consciousness experiences that we have carried into the present. They are held in our auric field.

4. *The soul level:* This level is all that we are.

Energy Testing

In order to find if a person has certain belief programs, we use a simple method called 'muscle testing' or 'energy testing.' Much like kinesiology, this tells us what programs the person does or does not have on the four levels we have just discussed.

Energy testing is a direct procedure in which the practitioner is testing the energy field or All That Is essence of a person. This originated from the conventional form of medical diagnostic kinesiology. It allows both the practitioner and the client to experience a reaction to a stimulus and gain physical and visual validation that a program exists. The body must be properly hydrated for muscle testing to work. Once the body is properly hydrated, muscle testing is a useful tool. There are two distinct methods for energy testing in belief work.

ENERGY TESTING: METHOD ONE

Sit down opposite the client. With an up and down motion, move your hand in front of their chest, making a slicing motion downward and back up again. This will 'zip them up,' pulling their electromagnetic field together so that they will energy test correctly.

1. Have the client put their thumb and either their forefinger or ring finger together in a circle. Tell them to hold their fingers together tightly.

2. Instruct them to say 'I am a man' or 'I am a woman,' depending on gender, i.e. if they are a woman, prompt them to say 'I am a woman.'

3. Pull their fingers apart to gauge a 'strong' or 'weak' hold. The fingers should hold very tightly, indicating a strong, or 'yes,'

answer. If they come loosely apart, this indicates a weak, or 'no,' answer. This indicates they are dehydrated. Give them a glass of water.

ENERGY TESTING: METHOD TWO

There is another type of muscle test that you can use when healing yourself, with someone on the telephone, or even with clients who are in your presence.

1. While standing facing north, the person being tested should say, 'Yes.' Their body should lean forward for a positive answer.

2. When they say, 'No,' their body should lean backward, indicating a negative response.

3. If their body does not lean at all, they are likely to be dehydrated.

4. If they move forward on a 'no' answer or backward on a 'yes' answer, this also indicates dehydration.

5. Once the person leans toward north for 'yes' and leans backward for 'no,' they are ready to be tested for programs.

Digging

One of the ways in which a ThetaHealing practitioner can be more effective in a one-on-one session is to use something that is now called *digging*. Digging is energy testing for the key belief that holds many beliefs in place. The practitioner plays the role of investigator, hunting for the emotional issue that is the root cause of the beliefs that stem from it. As the practitioner energy tests the person, the statements made by the person will give clues to the key belief.

It is helpful to visualize the belief system as a tower of blocks. The bottom block is the *key belief* that is holding the rest of the beliefs up. Always ask the Creator, 'Which key belief is holding this belief system intact?' You can save hours of time by seeking and clearing the major key beliefs.

The process is easy! All you have to do is ask 'Who?', 'What?', 'Where?,' 'Why?', and 'How?' The client's mind will do the digging for you, accessing information like a computer, and will give you an answer to every question.

If they seem to get stuck while finding an answer, it is only temporary. Change the question from 'Why? to 'How?', etc., until an answer manifests itself. If there is no answer, ask, 'If you did know the answer, what would it be?' With a little practice, you will learn how to access the ability of the mind to find the answer. And at any time in the belief work process the Creator may come to you and give you the bottom belief that you are looking for, so be open to divine intervention.

As soon as you have the key belief, ask the Creator whether to release it, replace it, or simply delete some aspect of it. Never replace programs without proper discernment. What might at first be perceived as a negative program may actually be beneficial.

Digging does not, however, mean asking the Creator what to change and nothing more. It involves a discussion with the client, since the simple act of talking about the topic will free them from part of the issue. It will, in effect, bring the programs into the light of the conscious mind to be released spontaneously.

When replacing a program, the first thing you need to understand is which neuronal connection you need to work on. Then, once you have modified the synapses, you have to make sure that you change the associated patterns that might interfere with the new concept as well. Remember that historical beliefs and genes may also block the insertion of a new belief.

The key point is in the client–practitioner interaction, but the client must not focus too much on the idea that their brain has been reprogrammed, or the subconscious may attempt to replace the new program with the old one.

Always find out how the bottom belief has served the person and what they have learned from it. There is generally a positive aspect to most bottom beliefs, such as 'If I am overweight, my feelings are safe' or 'If I am overweight, my deepest feelings will stay hidden.' As you can see, our mind is always doing its best to protect us from pain. Making sure that a person understands why they have had a program that isn't for their highest and best will help them to avoid recreating the same energy.

It is always best to find the deepest program before the session has ended. Feeling work will help here, since in many instances the insertion of feelings will expedite the process of finding the deepest program.

Feeling Work

Many people do not know how to express love for a soul mate and this is because they have never developed those feelings. It is hard to attract a soul mate if you are unable to give back the love that is given.

Some people have never experienced the energy of certain feelings in their lives. Perhaps they were traumatized as a child and did not develop these feelings, or they lost them somewhere in the emotional drama-trauma of this existence.

Never having experienced what it feels like to be loved, for example, or be rich, is the reason why, when we want to manifest a soul mate, or abundance, the manifestations do not come about. In order to manifest what we want, we have to *experience* the feelings first. This shows us that there are possibilities in the universe and makes it possible for us to believe in them.

In order to experience what it feels like to be loved by someone, or any other feeling we may be unfamiliar with, we must be shown by the Creator.

To give a client the experience of a particular feeling, a ThetaHealing practitioner gets their verbal permission and connects with the Creator of All That Is. The practitioner then witnesses the energy of the feeling 'downloading' from the Creator into the person and flowing through every cell of their body and all four belief levels. In this way, what might otherwise take lifetimes to learn can be learned in seconds.

As with belief work, energy testing is used to ascertain what someone does not understand how to feel or what they do not know, using the following formats:

- 'I understand what it feels like to...'

- 'I know...'

- 'I know when...'

- 'I know how...'

- 'I know how to live my daily life...'

- 'I know the perspective of the Creator of All That Is on...'

- 'I know it is possible to...'

- 'I am...'

- 'I do...'

For example:

- 'I understand what it feels like to trust.'

- 'I know what it feels like to trust.'

- 'I know when to trust.'

- 'I know how to trust.'

- 'I know how to live my daily life trusting and being trustworthy.'

- 'I know the perspective of the Creator of All That Is on trust and how to trust.'

- 'I know it is possible to trust and be trustworthy.'

- 'I am trustworthy.'

- 'I do trust.'

Once the feeling has been experienced, the person is ready to create life changes. I have seen many lives changed simply by downloading feelings from the Creator.

In ThetaHealing, you can also be your own practitioner and do your own belief and feeling work.

Here's how to carry out the belief and feeling work process, including digging, presented as if you were working with another person:

THE FIVE STEPS OF BELIEF WORK AND THE EIGHT WAYS OF DIGGING

Step 1: Establish a bond of trust

- Make the client comfortable.

- Listen to what the client has to say. Acknowledge what they have to say and question them without being overly aggressive.

- It is important to make eye contact with the client. Watch the body language of the client. This will give an indication of when a sensitive point in the belief work discussion has been reached.

Step 2: Identify the issue

- Determine what issue (belief) the client would like to work on in the session. This is the surface belief that you will be working on to find the bottom belief.

- Identify how the belief is being expressed in a specific situation in the life of the client.

- Perform an energy test to determine what the client believes to be true.

- Set a common goal with the client: 'Let's delve deep into the issue together and get to the bottom of it.'

Step 3: Begin the digging process

Digging for the bottom belief that will release all the beliefs stacked above it is an art form. No two people are the same and it is important to note that each digging session is going to be different. There are eight common approaches to digging work. These are as follows:

1. Basic questions

- Start by asking the basic questions. These are:

    'Who?'

    'What?'

    'Where?'

    'Why?'

    'How?'

- Examples:

    'Why do you think so?'

'What did you learn from it?'

'How did it serve you?'

● If the person says, 'I don't know,' ask, 'What if you did know?' or 'But if you did know, what...?' This is an opening to deeper belief programs.

2. Phobias

● Identify the deepest fear that underlies all other fears. Ask:

'What is the worst thing that could happen if you were in a given situation?'

'What would happen next in that situation?'

3. Drama (trauma)

● Identify an incident in the past that first evoked the traumatic emotions such as anger, sadness, resentment, guilt, and refusal.

● Then identify the current indicators of the feelings of the person:

'When did you begin to feel that way?'

'Who do you feel that way toward?'

'Where were you when you began to feel that way?'

'What was happening at that time?'

'How do you feel about the situation?'

'What action would you like to take from the feelings you are having about the situation?'

● Identify when the feeling evolved:

'When was the first time you were in a similar situation and experienced a similar feeling?'

'How did you feel then?'

- Witness the beliefs being released and changed on the four levels of belief (core, genetic, history, and soul).

- Download the feelings that are needed to help the person to recognize the bottom belief.

- Ask:

    'What did you learn from that experience?'

    'Why did you have to experience that?'

    'How did it serve you and how does it continue to serve you?'

4. Sickness

- Find out what the issues are and then start digging deeper.

- Find out why the person became sick:

    'When did the illness start?'

    'What was going on in your life at that time?'

- Find out why the person remains sick:

    'What is the best thing that has happened to you as a result of being sick?'

    'What have you learned from being sick?'

- Find out why the person cannot heal:

    'What would happen if you were healed completely?'

5. Manifesting

- Ask the client to visualize what they would do if they had all the money they wanted.

- Ask the client where they would be if they had all the money they wanted.

- How do they feel with all the money they ever wanted?

- Is there a significant other in the person's life, and if there is, how do they react to all that money and so forth? How do the person's family and friends react?

- Discover issues that make the client uncomfortable in their visualization and start digging deeper to resolve these issues. Ask:

    'What would you do if you had all the money you ever wanted?'

    'What could go wrong in that situation?'

6. Gene work

If you find, by muscle testing, that the person has certain beliefs that they do not consciously believe in, you may find that they become confused, making it difficult to continue your digging work. These beliefs may be their ancestors' beliefs that have been passed down to them.

- Continue digging by asking:

    'Is this your mother's belief?'

    'Is this your father's belief?'

    'Is this an ancestor's belief?'

7. Group consciousness beliefs

When many people have the same belief, they accept it as a fact and it becomes a group consciousness belief.

- Extract these beliefs and completely eliminate them so that the client can continue. If, for example, they believe:

    'Diabetes is incurable.'

'I am afraid of using my power.'

'I have taken a vow of poverty.'

● You can download:

'Diabetes is curable.'

'I can use my power safely and peacefully.'

'The vow of poverty is completely ended.'

8. The impossible

This work is performed not to find blocks but to reprogram the brain to accept what is currently perceived as impossible.

● Ask:

'What would happen if...?'

Step 4: Change the belief

● Perform healing on emotions that arise during the session.

● Replace the underlying belief with a positive belief.

● Present downloads to help support the new belief.

Step 5: Confirm that the belief has been changed

● Confirm that the belief has been change by performing energy testing.

Ask the Creator

The Creator is with you during belief work. You are never alone. Always ask for the Creator's help when you are lost and need some guidance.

Examples of things you can ask the Creator:

- which issue to focus on from multiple issues

- whether a specific belief is an underlying belief

- what the underlying belief is in a given situation

- which new belief will replace the old belief

- what questions you should ask when you are lost during a belief work session

- what feelings to download into the person to help a particular situation

Ask in the format:

Creator of All That Is, tell me the feelings to download for this person. Thank you! It is done, it is done, it is done.

Now you have the ThetaHealing tools to help you find love. We will return to belief work and how it can help you in Chapter 4. But first let's look at what love really is.

Chapter 2

LEVELS OF LOVE

To a large extent, our lives are filled with the search for love in all its shapes and forms, especially unconditional love. To find examples of this, we need only observe in ourselves and in others the driving need to have pets, to have friends, to find a soul mate, and to have children. This need begins in childhood and continues throughout our lives. Children want a 'best friend.' Women create tightknit social groups with other women. Men have 'male-bonding' sessions and practice or watch competitive sports to feel comradely toward one another. Both men and women are looking for that special love.

Most positive human relations are the result of this search. Even anger and hatred are the result of it. Why? Because there are a large number of people who have a difficult time finding love. This may be because they don't love themselves or because they have never experienced love, so don't understand what it is, even though they instinctually know that there is a level of feeling that is absent from their lives.

When I was a little girl, people always disappointed me when it came to love. I felt that they couldn't love me, because they didn't know how to love anything. I attempted to love *them* first, thinking that then perhaps they could reciprocate and learn to love me. Then I came to know that the reason why most people couldn't be good to you or be nice to you was that they didn't know *how* to love or know the *feeling* of love.

As a child, I also thought that loving other people meant seeing only the good parts of them, not the bad. This concept was taken from me later in life when the Law of Truth showed me the truth about people in the Akashic Records. That night I saw the deepest, darkest secrets of all the people in my life, and this unsettled me so much that I decided to disappear into the hills of Montana (which in a way I eventually did). Since I didn't have the money to move to Montana there and then, though, I was forced to confront the people about their secrets. So I began to learn what unconditional love really meant. I learned that to have unconditional love for people was to love them in 'Christ' or 'Buddha' consciousness, which was to see their truth through the Creator (or with enlightenment) and still love them in spite of it.

Such love is a wonderful thing, but loving people unconditionally doesn't mean that we should allow ourselves to be taken advantage of or allow difficult people into our lives. The search for enlightenment should not be confused with putting up with abuse simply so that we can say that we have unconditional love for people. It is important that this love is tempered with the additional knowledge that we are able to be strong yet loving. Not everyone is going to match the vibration of unconditional love and the people in our lives will always try to bring us to their vibrational level so that they can feel comfortable in themselves. Some people have a lower vibration and are wallowing in hatred, anger, fear, and resentment. They 'dwell in darkness.' These kind of people will always attempt to bring others down to their level of reality. But those who are in the light need only let it shine and others will come to it of their own accord.

It has been my experience that negative programs associated with unconditional love are generally created in childhood. For instance, a mother might show real love to her child one moment, only to mercilessly beat them immediately after. Or a father might express real love to a child and then molest them. It is because of childhood situations such as this that people don't know how to receive unconditional love.

Real unconditional love is best shared with someone who knows what it is. A compatible soul mate will have learned how to have unconditional love in a relationship.

Love between two people still has conditions to it, however, no matter how spiritually evolved you might be. If someone tells you that they want to be loved unconditionally, this generally means that they want have a relationship without rules. In order for two people to be in a relationship, though, there have to be ground rules that both follow, or there would be no point in being together in a pair bond.

Many people are generous by nature and have a tendency to give to others all the time. Because of this, they will draw soul mates to them who are not generous and take more energy from the relationship than they give. Be certain that you are ready for a soul mate to give you back the love that you give. Always make sure that you can accept and receive joy and that you can accept and receive love.

In order to find the love that you need, it is important to define just what love means to you. As with many other topics, it may be that the way that you perceive love is not for your highest and best. Be open to exploring the many facets of love and what it means to you. Love has many levels.

THE LEVELS OF LOVE

These are the levels of love as they relate to manifesting soul mates:

1. Love of God

2. Love of self

3. Love between two people: true love

4. Love of family

5. Love of friends

6. Love of community, all God's creatures, and the universe

7. Unconditional love

1. Love of God

It is important that we have a healthy love for the Creator. This has vast possibilities. Throughout history, humankind has been on a quest to perceive God, who has taken on many forms, shapes, and styles, depending on individual and cultural conceptions. Even in a single lifetime, our perception of the Creator is constantly changing and growing, depending on the many influences from the household, external society, religion, and more recently, modern science.

For the standpoint of this book, God is the highest aspiration of us all, the light of truth that each of us strives to bring forth in ourselves. And the light of God transcends our immoralities and human inconsistencies with the loving forgiveness of acceptance.

Of course there are those who choose not to believe in God. Our limited understanding of the Creator's loving essence may cause this misunderstanding. Many people also see themselves in an 'angry child–oppressive parent' relationship with God. Some blame all the difficult things in their lives on God, just as some children do with their parents. This is only one of many scenarios relating to God that people waste their precious energy on.

It is important to explore how you feel about God, since this is also how you feel about yourself. The reason that I say this is because I feel that we are divine sparks of God, and this makes us a part of the divine essence of God. Accepting this concept makes us behave with greater consideration toward ourselves and others.

This is why it is important to explore how you feel about the subject of God, and what your beliefs are concerning God. Once you have released and replaced negative beliefs about God, then you can move on to learn how to 'love thyself.'

2. Love of Self

Love of self comes when you learn to connect with the Creator. And when you love yourself, you forgive what you perceive as your shortcomings. Self-forgiveness is all-important, as it relates to self-growth. Becoming well-adjusted and in balance with your inner world is a vital stage on the path of self-discovery.

Loving yourself also means that you don't permit others to take advantage of you. You learn how to say 'no' to the people in your life who are not for your highest and best.

Here again it is important to explore how you feel about yourself and what your deep-seated beliefs about yourself are. These are the first two steps toward manifesting your compatible soul mate.

3. Love between Two People: True Love

Real love doesn't happen every day. It is an amazing treasure when two people love one another in the same way. True love is precious and it is difficult to replace. You can never find the same true love in another person, so don't think you can. It is precious, so treat it that way.

True love is what this book is dedicated to. It will be fully discussed throughout the book.

4. Love of Family

On this plane, love of family is established when we love our parents, our siblings, and our children. For some healers, love of family is difficult because while they can easily love their children, their siblings may be so different from them that they may find it difficult to like and love them. For instance, you may not *like* your sister but it is important to remember that you love her, or you may like your sister but it may be difficult to *love* her. For some healers, unconditional love for a stranger may be easier than love for their own family because of sibling competition and abuse from childhood.

To learn to like and love siblings and work through differences from a lifetime is important in order to be able to love those who are not your siblings. Many people take their whole lives to balance these issues with family and most resolve them only later on in life.

5. Love of Friends

Love of friends is when you create relationships with devoted friends. These are people you can love, be there for, and communicate with. Loving friends is also a way to progress emotionally toward spiritual goals.

6. Love of Community, All God's Creatures, and the Universe

Love of community is when you love the people who are in your area and are part of your culture. This can include those of your religion and your ethnic origin. In order to progress spiritually, however, we must have the capacity to love the people of the world as a whole. Then this love will expand to include the creatures of the world, the people and creatures of other planets, and finally the whole universe.

7. Unconditional Love

Unconditional love is seeing the truth about everyone and everything but still having love for them.

In order to progress spiritually, it is important to balance out all these kinds of love and achieve peace before we leave this plane.

To discover your own beliefs about love, try the following exercise:

BELIEFS ABOUT LOVE

You may want a relationship in which the other person will love and cherish you, but be reminded that you must know how to return this love. So check whether you can both love and be loved:

● Energy test for the program: 'To be loved, I have to be needed by others.'

● If you test positive for this program, reaffirm in yourself:

'I know how to have balance with love.'

'I love myself.'

'It is safe to be loved.'

'I love God and God loves me.'

● Energy test for the following beliefs:

'I believe I can be loved by another person.'

'I can receive love from another person.'

'There is no one out there for me.'

'I know how to return the love that is given to me.'

● See if you understand what it feels like to be surrounded by people you can love and whose love you can return – intelligent, uplifting individuals who build your spirit and help you soar and for whom you do the same in return.

● Instill (or download) what this feels like with the following command:

> 'Creator of All That Is, it is commanded that I understand what it feels like to be surrounded by people who love me.'

● See if you understand the Creator's definition of what it feels like to be surrounded by intelligent, uplifting individuals who build your spirit and help you soar and for whom you do the same in return.

● Bring in the feeling and knowing of love from the Creator on every level – physically, mentally, emotionally, and spiritually – by downloading these feelings of love from the Creator:

'I understand the Creator's definition of love.'

'I understand the Creator's definition of love for my human body.'

'I understand what it feels like to allow someone to love me.'

'I understand what it feels like to have discernment and love.'

'I know the Creator's definition of marriage.'

'I know the Creator's definition of intimacy.'

'I know the Creator's definition of trusting a soul mate.'

'I know the Creator's definition of loving a soul mate.'

'I know it is possible to be worthy of the love of a compatible soul mate.'

'I know I am worthy of having a compatible soul mate.'

'I know how to live without being needlessly jealous.'

These downloads should be offered to your partner to help them be more compatible to you.

Chapter 3

A GUIDE TO
SOUL MATES

One of the reasons why we have come into this incarnation is to understand all kinds of love – to master the virtues of love. One of these is the complete love of a partner. This is a relationship in which we learn how to love another person intimately, totally, and completely. In order to do this, we need the right kind of soul mate.

So, what exactly is a soul mate? There are several ideas out there.

To most people, a soul mate is someone they knew in another time and place, possibly a past life of some kind. In this past life, a deep emotional attachment was developed that transcended the physical. The memory of this attachment somehow survived the cleansing process of death and was reborn into this life. Some people believe that a soul mate is anyone we have ever loved in another place and time.

There are soul-mate relationships like this. We have all been reincarnated from past lives or, to coin a better term, *pre-existences*. Some of us have dim memories of the past before life. We may meet our soul mate and recognize that we are still in love with them. We may not remember all that happened in the past, but the feelings of love are immediate and deep.

There are various belief systems with shared themes about reincarnated lovers. The Hindu religion is one, but there are others that are subtler, hidden from plain sight in Western culture.

If we instantly recognize someone, however, we could also know them from the spirit world, or they could be what people call 'heaven-sent with a purpose.'

Also, a union of souls is not necessarily a reunion of spirits from a past time. Brand-new, spiritual soul-mate unions are being made in the here and now, and the energy of these unions shines out, giving hope to others in exactly the same way as a reunion of spirits does. To the people involved in this kind of union, a soul mate is someone they are dreaming into life right now, and they aren't concerned with past lives.

I believe that a soul mate can be someone who, by their disposition, personality, spiritual and physical form, is attuned to us for some reason, and this attunement may have nothing to do with past lives and everything to do with physical, mental, emotional, and spiritual attraction that is ignited for the first time.

This concept removes us from the much more spiritual aspects of reincarnation that some people find impractical. Many people, by their nature, simply want to be with someone in a meaningful relationship, a bond that lasts for life. Why they feel the need for this kind of relationship is not important to them, nor do they attempt to explain it using spiritual terms. What *is* important to them is finding that special person with whom they feel safe and comfortable. If you are this kind of person, this book will still benefit you, since you may be blocking yourself in ways that you don't fully realize.

To many people, a divine mate just seems too much to ask of the world. They believe it is unobtainable – and so it is. Others (who are more analytical) become confused by the phrase 'soul mate.' They have no idea what this inexplicable term means, because it is beyond their experience.

But what if you have many different soul mates out there in the world? What if each one of these soul mates is by their nature someone you could fall in love with? You may say that many of us fall in love more than once, and we do. Many of us want that one special person to be with, but find that we fall deeply in love with more than one person during our life.

I believe that this feeling about a 'special person' is the right one, but I also think that we fall in love more than once because we have more than one soul mate. These 'transitional' soul mates don't always have to be someone we knew in a past life. They can be someone who by their nature has something to teach us, possibly someone we are drawn to because we share more of their negative beliefs than positive ones. I call these kind of soul mates 'spiritual carrots' that lead us to the right one! This refers to a boy sitting on a cart being pulled by a donkey. He holds a long stick to which a carrot has been tied that is just out of reach of the donkey. As the donkey moves forward to take the carrot, it pulls the cart forward, just as a transitional soul mate draws us forward to a compatible one.

This may be why other people are drawn to us, too. It is also why it is so important that we do belief work on ourselves so that we can be ready for our divine life-partner soul mate.

How can we distinguish all these soul mates? I have found that there are seven essential classifications of soul mate and one group called a soul family.

SOUL FAMILY MEMBERS

Soul families and soul mates are people whose spirits we recognize from other places and times. We seem to know them and can read their minds easily. The difference between a soul family and a soul mate is that a soul family member is related to you on a spiritual level and a soul mate is not.

A soul family is exactly as it sounds: the spiritual family that we belonged to before we came into this incarnation. I believe that we have experienced many planes of existence before this life and one of these existences was when we were part of a soul family on the Fifth Plane of Existence.

Soul family members descend as individuals to inhabit physical families on this plane with missions to heal the planet or to accumulate virtues, but somehow they never forget the spiritual family that they left behind. Have you ever felt as though you are in the wrong family and there is another one that you really belong to? This may be why you have these feelings.

Soul families have a tendency to travel through time together in different incarnations, so some family members will incarnate at the same time and meet one another. In some instances their feelings and memories will bring them together in matrimony. But because they are part of the same soul family, there is no lasting passion between them. It is like a brother and a sister marrying without knowing it.

ThetaHealing is designed to bring soul families together once again. Soul families are our eternal spiritual support system and they are being drawn together to do the work of the Creator here on Earth. Every soul family has a Council of Twelve presiding over it, guiding and aiding its members. These councils are held on the higher degrees of the Fifth Plane and many masters who are here on missions from the Fifth Plane are rising up out of their space when they are asleep to take part in them. (For more on this, see *The Seven Planes of Existence*.)

In terms of a relationship, the difference between a soul mate and a soul family member is that a soul family member has particular spiritual energies that we have experienced before in a non-sensual and non-sexual way with a brotherly or sisterly love. So, if you are drawn to someone and feel they are very familiar, but you realize that you are not compatible with them, they might be a soul brother or sister or soul friend.

A soul mate is different in that there is a sensual and sexual attraction between you, as well as a mental and spiritual magnetism. Some soul mates have been in passionate love with each other through many planes of existence. Throughout time, there has been a lasting passion between them.

SOUL MATES

The seven types of soul mate are:

1. The twin flame

   A twin flame is someone who is exactly like you.

2. The incompatible soul mate

   An incompatible soul mate is a soul you have known before. Because of this, you have an emotional and physical attraction to them, but they are nonetheless incompatible with you.

3. The 'diamond in the rough' soul mate

   This is a soul mate who can be compatible with you, but you have met them before they have developed enough for a relationship.

4. The unfinished business soul mate

   These are soul mates who have unfinished business from a past-life relationship. They have the opportunity to meet again and repair the karma between them.

5. The compatible soul mate

These are soul mates who are perfect for now but may grow apart.

6. The compatible life soul mate

These are compatible soul mates with an added spiritual connection.

7. The divine life-partner soul mate

A divine life-partner soul mate is someone who shares your divine timing – your mission in this life on Earth.

Let's look at all these soul mates in a bit more depth.

1. The Twin Flame

Some people are confused when looking for a soul mate and ask the Creator for a twin flame instead. A twin flame is someone who is exactly like you, and this may cause much friction between the two of you. They may also be a mirror of the way you were 20 years ago, with all the maturity of an 18-year-old. This is not likely to be a long-lasting relationship. Most of the time, when we meet a twin flame, they only stay in our life a little while.

2. The Incompatible Soul Mate

An incompatible soul mate is someone you have known in another time or place. It is easy to fall in love with this kind of soul mate, as you remember how much you loved each other before. Nevertheless, the two of you now have a completely different vibration. You have become incompatible.

An incompatible soul mate can, however, be a 'carrot' to guide you to your compatible soul mate, because they will teach you the qualities that you want in a soul mate. The universe is using someone to take you from a difficult situation to a better one.

3. The 'Diamond in the Rough' Soul Mate

A diamond in the rough soul mate is one who has all the qualifications to be a truly compatible soul mate, but is not yet fully developed.

If you have met your soul mate before they are fully developed, this means that, just like an uncut diamond, it is going to take some work to bring out their clarity, quality, and brilliance. It will take time and patience for you to be compatible. So it is important to ask the universe: 'When will my soul mate be ready for me?' This question is especially important if you are looking for your divine soul mate.

Had I met Guy 10 years before I did, neither of us would have been ready for the relationship. Guy wasn't ready for me five years before we met. I'm not even sure that he was fully ready for me when we did meet. He was my diamond in the rough, and boy, was he rough! He had been out on the ranch for years and only went to town if it was absolutely necessary. And he didn't know how to have a quiet voice. This was because his father was partly deaf and he had to speak loudly to be heard. The man who gets in front of classes these days had to train to modulate his voice, and it took years for him to do that. I would tell him, 'Guy, you are scaring the ladies in the class.' He couldn't sit still either, because he was used to doing manual labor. Emotionally, we were ready for one another, but only barely.

So, have patience. What if the universe is assisting the development of your soul mate so that they will be ready for you when you meet them? You might want to meet them now, but meeting them before they are ready will only mean that the two of you will be incompatible. Perhaps your soul mate is like a cake that is baking in the oven. If you take them out too soon, they will collapse.

Many of us are so powerful in our manifestations that in our arrogance and impatience we bring our soul mate to us before they are ready. A friend of mine manifested her soul mate, but there was one little problem – he was in the middle of a divorce. So she had to experience the emotional drama of a man going through a divorce. This kind of situation is not conducive to a smooth relationship.

4. The Unfinished Business Soul Mate

A *master* is a spiritual being who, over many lifetimes, has accumulated enough virtues to move up beyond this third-dimensional reality to what I call the Fifth Plane of Existence. If at any time they come back to this third-dimensional reality, they are known as an *ascended master*. Many ascended masters have recently returned to this Earth to inhabit human bodies and to tutor the *children of the masters* who are living on this planet. Generally, they come back on a mission to help humanity.

Because ascended masters have been here many times in different incarnations, they have the opportunity to meet souls they have known in other times and places. These might be from their soul families on the Fifth Plane or they might be from past lives.

If the masters have any unresolved energy with any of these souls, when they meet again they will have the opportunity to clear the issues between them. However, when a master meets someone and gets the feeling that something needs to be cleared, it isn't compulsory for them to do so. It is a voluntary thing and the issue needs to be cleared by the other person, too.

Children of the masters, who make up the rest of the soul population of Earth, have been sent to this plane to learn and grow. They are third-dimensional beings and live many lifetimes resolving the karma of negative lifetimes. They also may have unfinished business from a past-life relationship. If so, they will have an opportunity to meet the person again in their next life and repair the karma between them. In many instances, people get into relationships to correct karma, and when it has been cleared, they outgrow the relationship and move on.

This explains why some of us have more than one soul mate in a lifetime. For example, I have been married four times. (Yes, I have a husband for every direction!) Part of the reason I married these people was because, on a higher level, there was unresolved energy with them from another time and place. This doesn't necessarily mean that there was unfinished business on just my part; it may have been more on the part of the other person.

Part of the reason I was divorced from three of these men was because this unfinished energy between us was resolved. The other reason that these people came into my life was because every experience in life matters on a level that we may not at first fully understand. Each one of them taught me things about myself and helped me to a higher consciousness. Difficult as some of the relationships were, in their own way they helped me to awaken as a spiritual person.

5. The Compatible Soul Mate

A compatible soul mate is someone who loves and understands you. They are compatible with your personality, but this doesn't mean that they are easy to be with. Healers in particular never seem to be compatible with someone who is too 'easy', because they seem to get 'easily' bored. They need someone who will engage with them, talk to them, interact with them, and stimulate them.

Also, a compatible soul mate is someone who is compatible with who you are right now. They are compatible with the vibration you are holding at this particular time in your life. That's fine, but you may grow spiritually in leaps and bounds, so you may want to ask for someone who will grow with you – a compatible life soul mate.

6. The Compatible Life Soul Mate

A compatible life soul mate or compatible life partner is someone who goes through your life with you and grows with you spiritually and mentally. They share more positive beliefs with you than negative ones and are drawn to you because of this. They encourage your growth as a person.

One of the goals that we have as a soul in this existence is to find a life partner to be with or to find true love with that special person who follows us from existence to existence.

Compatible life soul mates have a deep affinity for each other and are suited to each other temperamentally. It may be that some of their interests are different, but the bond that they have is of a divine nature.

A union of two people who are harmonious in their dispositions, points of view, sensitivity to each other and to the world around them creates an energy that is palatable, poignant, and lasting beyond this life.

It is my belief that a compatible life soul mate is someone who for some inexplicable reason knows you totally and completely in a way words cannot easily express. To me, this is what a soul mate should be. When you meet them, you recognize them immediately as someone you have known before, but you don't know why. There is be a feeling of *déjà vu*, as though you have experienced these circumstances before. You appreciate the way they move, you recognize the energy that flashes from their eyes. It seems to come from another place and time. And along with this soul recognition, you have a strong and intense attraction to them. These spiritual feelings are not easily explained in the written word.

A soul-mate relationship is all about the energy of a person. We are attracted to their energy as much as we are to their looks. We are drawn to them just like a magnet. The soul is magnetic in nature, much like the Earth's magnetic field. We are a small world unto ourselves and we are magnetically attracted to those who are the opposite in polarity, not only (usually) because of their gender, but also because of their vibration. When you are manifesting a soul mate, you should manifest being attracted to an energy that is equal to your own or even a little higher than your own.

Be extremely careful when you ask for a soul mate. Know exactly what you are asking for so that you will recognize the person when you find them (more on this later), and always ask for one who is *compatible* with you.

That won't be one who is perfect for you in every way. Any relationship is an energy that requires stimulation and a lot of give and take to keep it alive. That is another reason why you need to be prepared for a soul mate to come into your life.

There is a proper way to go about finding your most compatible life soul mate, and that is by allowing them to find you and allowing the universe to serve you. I know many people cannot find their soul mates simply because they are looking too hard.

When you truly know and love yourself, you are ready for a compatible life soul mate, but that doesn't mean that they are ready for you. We are all evolving at different speeds. However, I believe that there is someone out there for everyone.

Right before you find your most compatible life soul mate you will have an overwhelming and foreboding sense of loneliness. This is a good indicator that a special someone is around the corner.

But remember that any soul mate, even a compatible one, only complements you. No one can make you complete; you must be complete on your own. If you are not a whole person in and of yourself, you have nothing to bring to a relationship.

7. The Divine Life-Partner Soul Mate

The divine life-partner soul mate, or divine soul mate, is more than a compatible soul mate. They are someone who has mastered this existence before and shares their divine timing, their mission in this incarnation, with their mate. My current soul-mate relationship is with my divine life partner. I say this because he shares my vision and has the same divine timing as I do. This also means that he won't interfere with my divine timing.

Everyone on this Third Plane has a divine timing, a purpose, for each lifetime. It is what we have come here to accomplish. Many of us have come to master virtues and others have come to change the course of the planet's evolution in some way.

A child of the masters generally masters several virtues in a lifetime and carries them to the next in a constant spiral of learning from life to life until they ascend to the Fifth Plane and escape this third dimension.

The divine timing of a master is different in that they are here to elevate the consciousness of the children. They are each here to stimulate the consciousness of 10 to 15 children who will then go forth to change the consciousness of millions of people.

Some people can accomplish their divine timing mission by themselves. But many of us have the feeling that we don't want to be alone. Do you know why? We weren't meant to accomplish our mission alone. We were meant to accomplish it with the help and support of a special person. This means that part of our mission is to learn to give our love to one person completely.

Many masters have a divine life partner who helps them to achieve their life purpose. Some have made agreements to do something special in this life. With these people, it is their reason for being. Anyone who steps in the way of their mission will be moved out of the way, and that includes soul mates who do not share the vision.

Most people of a spiritual nature aren't looking for a compatible life soul mate, but someone to share their divine timing with. Obviously, this is one special person. Sometimes, finding them can be a tricky business. But when two souls have been together as Fifth-Plane beings, they will look for each other when they go into a human incarnation. There is one particular energy signature that they are searching for. They seem to know what that person looks like, and if they share the same path it is almost inevitable that they will meet.

I know that Guy and I have been assigned to be together and share a mission. I believe that when we met, the heavens opened up and we remembered each other and fell in love all over again. I also think that fairies or angels in the heavens watch over us so that we can accomplish our divine timing. Each time that we get in a fight, the alarm goes off, telling the fairies that it is time for the heavens to open up to sprinkle us with love dust again and we forget what we are fighting about. I believe that when we pass on from this life we will find out how many times we've been 'sprinkled' – probably hundreds of times!

Chapter 4

SOUL-MATE
BELIEF WORK

One day I was doing a reading with a beautiful woman who complained to me that no man would want her because she had five kids. She said, 'Who would want the responsibility of five kids?'

The next reading I did that same day was with a handsome man who was complaining about his life, and this is what he told me: 'I've spent my life becoming financially stable and I've missed the joy of a family. I need a nice woman who has children and may be interested in having more. Can you tell me how to find her?'

I thought to myself, She just walked out the door!

Each of these people had what the other wanted, but they couldn't meet because they didn't believe that such a person existed. If you think that finding a soul mate is impossible, that special person could be standing right in front of you and you'll still never meet them because of your *beliefs*.

Belief work was beginning to develop when Guy and I got together. Because of the issues that came up between us, it was in part designed so that we could have a successful relationship. It has saved my marriage many times, because I didn't know how to be married.

Part of the reason for this was the rather traumatic situations I'd been in in past relationships. I liked the idea of marriage, but I didn't know how to receive love. Because of this, the people I was in relationships with would always fall short of what I expected. When I downloaded what it felt like to receive love from a man, I realized that every one of the men in my life had loved me, but I'd been unable to accept their love.

I think this was because the way they acted toward me wasn't what I expected. One of the greatest challenges in relationships is that we don't tell the other person what we expect from them, we just expect them to know and to act upon it. And of course they don't know!

Many of us may have deep-seated programs and beliefs that are working against us finding a soul mate. This means that we're always looking for a soul mate but never manifest one because we're subconsciously blocking ourselves from ever finding one.

Another scenario is that we do actually find a soul mate, but don't want to live with them. Do you know how hard it is to live with another person, particularly if you've lived by yourself for a while? They are going to scratch their butt and burp when they eat!

If you have hidden programs and you are in a relationship with someone, it may be difficult to maintain a successful relationship because you will fight the person or create a scenario of sabotage so that they won't get too close. What if you let your guard down and then they leave you? What if they die, leaving you alone?

Don't feel bad if you have these feelings. Most people have them. Many people who are looking for a soul mate would rather look than find one. Others have hidden belief systems that stop them before they even start.

SOUL-MATE BELIEFS

Here are some beliefs to energy test for relating to sex, relationships, self-image, and soul mates. Understand that these beliefs are a baseline for others that you may have hidden in your subconscious mind. It may be that these other beliefs will reveal themselves in the belief work process and they may be genetic in nature.

Replace the beliefs that aren't serving you with those that are positive in nature. For example, replace 'I need to be needed to feel protected' with 'I am protected.' (There is a short guide to belief and feeling work in Chapter 1. For a more detailed guide, refer to *ThetaHealing* and *Advanced ThetaHealing*.)

In many instances, your subconscious mind will begin to replace these old beliefs automatically once it understands that they do not serve you.

Sex

Beliefs to muscle test for:

- 'My power is owned by others.'

- 'I am owned by others.'

- 'I have to have sex in order to feel beautiful.'

- 'I have to refrain from sex to feel safe.'

- 'It's safe to show my emotions when I'm sexual.'

- 'Sex is evil – dirty.'

- 'I am a sexual sacrifice.'

- 'I have to give up my body to appease others.'

- 'I use my body to hurt myself and to hurt others.'

- 'I have to cut myself to know I can feel – that I'm alive.'

- 'I can only feel sexual pleasure if I'm hurt.'

- 'I have to stay frozen to be sexual.'

- 'I have to be submissive in being sexual.'

- 'I have to be dominant in being sexual.'

- 'I can never be sexually satisfied.'

- 'I use my body as a shield against the invasion of others.'

- 'I have to have sex all the time.'

- 'It is my duty to have sex.'

- 'It's okay to show emotions during sex.'

- 'Men only want me for sex.'

- 'Women only want me for sex.'

- 'Sex is bad.'

- 'Sex is evil.'

- 'Sex is love.'

- 'Intimacy and sex are the same.'

- 'I am a victim.'

- 'It's wrong to have sex.'

- 'I can be with a sexual partner and be close to God.'

- 'Being loved brings a surge of hormones in my body.'

- 'It's okay to feel sensual and sexy and still have good discernment.'

- 'I deserve a soul mate.'

- 'No matter what I do, it is impossible to find my soul mate.'

- 'I have to be a virgin for someone to want me.'

- 'I am unclean because I have had sex.'

Self-image

- 'I am ugly.'

- 'I have ugly hair.'

- 'I have ugly teeth.'

- 'I have an ugly body.'

- 'I am alone in the world.'

- 'I am uninteresting.'

- 'I am too emotional for someone to understand me.'

- 'I know myself.'

- 'I complain all the time.'

- 'I know what I want in a mate.'

- 'I want people who are out of my reach.'

- 'No one I like is attracted to me.'

- 'I am attracted to difficult men.'

- 'I am attracted to difficult women.'

- 'Men only want me for money.'

- 'Women only want me for money.'

- 'I attract abusive men.'

- 'I attract abusive women.'

- 'Wild women are the most interesting.'

- 'Wild men are the most interesting.'

- 'I get bored with nice women.'

- 'I get bored with nice men.'

- 'I get bored with one person.'

- 'Passionate people are difficult.'

- 'If I am happy in a relationship, I will die.'

- 'I hate sharing money with a new mate.'

- 'Money is always a problem.'

- 'I must be independent in all I do.'

- 'It is safer to be alone.'

- 'I am stronger being alone.'

- 'No one will see me.'

- 'No one will love me.'

- 'When I am in love with someone, they own me.'

- 'I am a slave in relationships.'

- 'I am compulsive in relationships.'

- 'No one can love me enough.'

- 'I smother my mates.'

- 'I am over-jealous in my relationships.'

- 'If I fall in love, I will never recover.'

- 'A lover is too demanding.'

- 'I hate intimacy.'

- 'I hurt anyone who loves me.'

- 'To be close to God, I must be alone.'

- 'I have to lose weight.'

- 'I deserve a mate who is stable.'

- 'I must dominate my partner.'

- 'My romantic partner will attempt to control me.'

- 'My romantic partner will attempt to control my friends.'

- 'My friends will attempt to steal my mate.'

- 'I am drawn to mentally ill people.'

- 'Mentally ill people are drawn to me.'

- 'Romantic relationships end in tragedy.'

- 'My relationships are like my parents.'

- 'My relationships end in divorce.'

- 'My partner will cheat on me.'

- 'I am drawn to incompatible people.'

- 'I am drawn to people like my father.'

- 'I am drawn to people like my mother.'

- 'I am drawn to people like my ex-husband/ex-wife/ ex-partner.'

- 'I am drawn to unstable people.'

- 'I am married to my parents.'

- 'All women are the same.'

- 'All men are the same.'

- 'All women are cheats.'

- 'All men are cheats.'

- 'I hate the opposite sex.'

- 'I hate men.'

- 'I hate women.'

- 'I am a misandrist [man-hater].'

- 'I am a misogynist [woman-hater].'

- 'I hate relationships.'

- 'I want to avoid sharing my children.'

- 'My family will destroy my relationship.'

- 'My children will destroy my relationship.'

- 'Men will accept my children.' (If you have children.)

- 'Women will accept my children.' (If you have children.)

- 'My feelings about my past relationships are stable.'

- 'There is no one out there for me.'

- 'Good men will come to me.'

- 'Good women will come to me.'

- 'There are plenty of wonderful people out there.'

- 'Someone can love me.'

- 'I can receive love from another person.'

- 'Beautiful men are shallow.'

- 'Beautiful women are shallow.'

- 'I am complete without my soul mate.'

Fear

- 'I am afraid of sharing my whole being with another person.'

- 'I am afraid to let someone know me.'

- 'I am afraid to let someone love me.'

- 'I am afraid of giving too much.'

- 'I am afraid to start again.'

- 'I am too old to find love.'

- 'I am afraid of taking care of another person.'

- 'I want my soul mate to love me just for myself.'

- 'I have something to offer a lasting relationship.'

- 'I am loveable.'

- 'It's impossible for someone else to love me.'

- 'God lets me down when I get my hopes up.'

- 'I punish myself for my mistakes.'

- 'I have to give up who I am in order to be in a relationship.'

- 'I have to give up my identity in order to be in a relationship.'

Resentment

- 'I resent not being able to be with my most compatible soul mate.'

- 'My soul mate has come too late in my life and I'm with somebody else.'

- 'I resent having to be with somebody besides my soul mate.'

- 'I resent having to be alone to complete my life's mission.'

- 'I resent not being with my soul mate because soul mates are a lie – there's nobody out there for me.'

Tragedy

- 'Relationships end in tragedy.'

- 'If I love someone completely, there will be a tragedy.'

- 'If I find my soul mate, there will be a tragedy.'

- 'True love ends in tragedy.'

Energetic Divorce from Past Relationships

Many people have the hidden belief that they are married to another person, even when they are separated or physically divorced from them. This belief can be deep in the subconscious mind, which still believes that this program is a fine thing to have!

You don't have to be married to a person to be deeply attached to them in this way. Many people become so attached to someone that on an unconscious level they believe they are married to them, even when there is no binding physical contract or ceremony between them.

You'd be surprised how many people haven't severed their energetic commitment to a past love. Energy test for the beliefs below as they relate to marriage. Particularly if you've been divorced, energy test to see if you feel free of a commitment to a prior mate. Energy test to see if you are married to your family, your ex-boy/girlfriend or an ex-spouse. In your mind, make a list of everyone in your social circle. Even your commitment to your parents and children can be perceived by the unconscious mind as a marriage vow, and this needs to be released so that you can bring a romantic relationship into your life. Look at all your past relationships and your energetic attachment to them.

If you energy test that you are married to God, release this energy and replace it with healthy beliefs about God and your church. For instance, you should feel a love for God and church that still leaves room for you to have a soul mate.

The following are suggestions for replacing the old energy with new beliefs. While they may not be for you, they will give you an idea of what to replace the old energy with.

- 'I am married to God.'
  Replace with: 'I am connected to God.'

- 'I am married to my church.'
  Replace with: 'I love my church.'

- 'I am married to my land [property, real estate, home, farm, etc].'
  Replace with: 'I give and receive healing from the land.'

- 'I am married to my house.'
  Replace with: 'I own my house in the highest and best way.'

- 'I am married to my children.'
  Replace with: 'I love my children in the highest and best way.'

- 'I am married to my parents.'
  Replace with: 'I love my parents in the highest and best way.'

- 'I am married to my ex-husband.'
  Replace with: 'I am free of my ex-husband.'

- 'I am married to my ex-wife.'
  Replace with: 'I am free of my ex-wife.'

- 'I am married to my ex-boyfriend.'
  Replaced with: 'I am free of my ex-boyfriend.'

- 'I am married to my ex-girlfriend.'
  Replace with: 'I am free of my ex-girlfriend.'

- 'I am married to a magical memory of my first love.'
  Replace with: 'I can love again.'

- 'I am married to my career.'
  Replace with: 'I understand how to create balance in my life in the highest and best way.'

FEELINGS AND DOWNLOADS

The following are some suggested feelings to download into yourself from the Creator. These feelings can change the way that you feel about yourself to make it easier to find a soul mate. Go up in the Seventh-Plane meditation (*page* 6) and ask for each download.

Issues of Intimacy

- 'I know how to be intimate.'

- 'I know what it feels like to be intimate.'

- 'I have the Creator's definition of intimacy.'

- 'I know how to be nurtured.'

- 'I know what it feels like to be nurtured.'

- 'I know how to be listened to.'

- 'I know what it feels like to be listened to.'

- 'I know how to listen to my soul mate.'

- 'I know what it feels like to listen to my mate.'

Relationships and Soul Mates

- 'I know what it feels like to live my daily life without being victimized.'

- 'I have the Creator's definition of what it feels like to receive and accept love from a soul mate.'

- 'It's okay to feel sexual, sensual, and sexy, and still have good discernment.'

- 'I have the Creator's definition of what it feels like to enjoy sex with my soul mate.'

- 'I know how to receive and accept love from a soul mate.'

- 'I know how to love myself.'

- 'I know how to communicate with someone I am in love with.'

- 'I understand the Creator's definition of a soul mate.'

- 'I know the Creator's definition of marriage.'

- 'I know the Creator's definition of trusting a soul mate.'

- 'I know the Creator's definition of loving a soul mate.'

- 'I know I am worthy of having a compatible soul mate.'

- 'I know it is possible to be worthy of the love of a compatible soul mate.'

- 'I know how to live without being jealous.'

- 'I know how to be the prize.'

- 'I understand what it feels like to have my most compatible soul mate.'

- 'I understand who is the right person for me.'

- 'It is possible to have a compatible soul mate.'

- 'I know the difference between true love and sexual attraction.'

- 'I am ready for my most compatible soul mate.'

- 'I know how to prepare for my soul mate.'

- 'I know how to live my daily life with another person.'

- 'I know the perspective of the Creator of All That Is on a soul mate.'

- 'I know it is possible to have a soul mate.'

- 'I know how to recognize my most compatible soul mate.'

- 'I will become a loving soul mate.'

- 'I understand how to leave energies from past relationships behind me.'

- 'I understand how to treat another person with respect.'

- 'I understand how to communicate with my partner.'

- 'I understand how to have a love for a partner that is inspired by the divine.'

- 'I know how to bring out the best in a person.'

- 'I know how to open my heart to the right person.'

- 'I know how to be dedicated in a relationship.'

- 'I know how to receive dedication from my soul mate.'

- 'I understand what it feels like to express my feelings to another person in a relationship.'

- 'I know when to express my feelings in a relationship.'

- 'I know how to express my feelings in a relationship.'

- 'I understand what it feels like to be seen as beautiful by my soul mate.'

- 'I know how to let my true beauty shine for that special someone.'

- 'I understand what it feels like to be cherished by another person.'

- 'I understand the definition of love through the Creator of All That Is.'

- 'I understand what it feels like to love a man/woman.'

- 'I understand the definition of being loved by my companion through the Creator of All That Is.'

- 'I understand what it feels like to be loved by my companion.'

- 'I know when to be loved by my companion.'

- 'I know how to be loved by my companion.'

- 'I know how to live my daily life being loved by my companion.'

- 'I know the Creator's perspective on being loved by my companion.'

- 'I know what it feels like to have a relationship based on love.'

- 'I know what it feels like to live without giving up who I am in order to be in a relationship.'

- 'I know what it feels like to live without having to give up my identity in order to be in a relationship.'

- 'I know how to love someone completely and wholly.'

- 'I know how to give love.'

- 'I know how to deal with confrontation in the highest and best way.'

- 'I know how to live without fearing life.'

- 'I know how to live without guilt in relationships.'

- 'I know it is possible to be loved by my companion.'

- 'I know how to be flexible in a relationship.'

- 'I understand what it feels like to be safe with a partner.'

- 'I know how to live with someone without dominating them.'

- 'I know how to have a relationship without replaying past relationships.'

- 'I know how to have a relationship without making someone my father.'

- 'I know how to have a relationship without making someone my mother.'

- 'I know how to maintain my relationship with my soul mate.'

- 'I understand what it feels like to love my soul mate for who they are.'

- 'I know how to love my soul mate for what, who and all they can be.'

- 'I understand what it feels like to be devoted to a soul mate.'

- 'I understand what it feels like to be heard by my soul mate.'

- 'I know how to bring my soul mate to their highest potential.'

- 'I know how to create abundance through the energy of my relationship with my soul mate.'

- 'I know what it feels like to share my whole being with another person.'

- 'I know how to create a soul mate in this lifetime.'

- 'I know how to have my most compatible divine life soul mate.'

- 'I know how to live my daily life without giving myself away – prostituting myself.'

- 'I know how to live without giving my power to others.'

- 'I know the difference between my feelings/thoughts/beliefs/opinions/ideas/behaviors and those of another.'

- 'I know how to separate my feelings/thoughts/beliefs/opinions/ideas/behaviors from those of another person.'

- 'I know what it feels like to be connected to myself.'

- 'I know what it feels like and how to be connected to others without using their energy inappropriately.'

- 'I have the Creator's definition of interdependency.'

- 'I know what it feels like and how to be interdependent.'

- 'I know what it feels like to be alive and feel without hurting myself in any way.'

- 'I know what it feels like, how to and when to be sexual in the highest and best way.'

- 'I know what it feels like to be safe to be sexual.'

- 'I understand how to honor my sexuality without feeling the need to give it away.'

- 'I know how to feel powerful in the highest and best way while being sexual.'

- 'I know what it feels like to feel balanced and enjoy being sexual.'

- 'I know that the Creator of All That Is protects me when I'm sexual.'

- 'I know what it feels like and how to be safe to show my emotions when I'm sexual.'

- 'I know how and when to express my thoughts and truths while being sexual in the highest and best way.'

- 'I know what it feels like and how to enjoy being sexual in the highest and best way.'

BELIEF WORK IN PRACTICE

The following is a transcript of a belief work session I conducted with a man in a class. It will give you an idea of the hidden beliefs that many people have about relationships.

Vianna: If you could manifest changes in your life and create your future, what would you create?

Man: *I would create a situation where I did a lot of traveling and teaching. I would also create books.*

Vianna: Do you see the content of these books?

Man: *No.*

Vianna: Do you see where you are traveling?

Man: *I see myself in England and India.*

Vianna: What else would you manifest?

Man: *Really beautiful homes.*

Vianna: Okay, so close your eyes and imagine yourself in one of those really beautiful houses. Imagine yourself living in that world of traveling and teaching and in your favorite house. What's the worst thing that could happen to you in this manifestation?

Man: *Having to leave the house when I'm traveling. There is a feeling of sadness coming up when I think of this.*

Vianna: So you have this beautiful house and you're traveling all over the world. Why are you sad?

Man: *I think it's because I believe the house is a peaceful sanctuary, but I have to leave it to do what I have to do.*

Vianna: So it's a *burden* to do all these things that you want to do?

Man: *No, I like it, but it's kind of a double-edged sword. I like doing the things, but when I'm off doing them I don't get to be in my sanctuary.*

Vianna: Okay, so what's the worst thing that would happen to you if you received this manifestation?

Man: *I don't understand. I'm just sitting in the house crying.*

Vianna: This manifestation isn't making you happy. Why isn't it making you happy?

Man: *I don't know.*

Vianna: Close your eyes and put yourself back into the manifestation. What does everybody around you think about this success of yours? How do they feel about it?

Man: *They feel disconnected from me.*

Vianna: Have you disconnected yourself from them?

Man: *That's right, I have.*

Vianna: Are you lonely in that big beautiful house?

Man: *Yes, I guess so.*

Vianna: Is that why you're crying? Close your eyes and think for a minute. You have two beautiful houses to take care of and you are traveling. What does it feel like to be in this reality?

Man: *It feels lonely.*

Vianna: So you're lonely. There's no one there to share it with?

Man: *I'm not seeing anybody for me, sorry.*

Vianna: So, does this mean that the people who are in your life now are no longer in your life? Have they disconnected from you completely because of your success?

Man: *It feels as though most of them can't relate to me anymore.*

Vianna: Do you want these people in your life?

Man: *Some of them.*

Vianna: Have you lost all of them or just a few of them?

Man: *I've lost some of them. Some of them are still around, but they have their own lives and don't have time for me.*

Vianna: You're living your dream, but you're lonely. Repeat after me: 'If I live my dream, I will be lonely.'

Man: *If I live my dream, I will be lonely.* [He energy tests 'yes.']

Vianna: It seems that you have this program. Repeat after me: 'If I have abundance, I will be lonely.'

Man: *If I have abundance, I will be lonely.* [He energy tests 'yes.']

Vianna to the students in the class: I'm not pulling any of these programs at this time, I'm only talking to him about them. If I just start pulling them at random, I'm never going to find the bottom belief. [*To man:*] So now we have something to go on. What I'm going to do now is find out why you feel this way. Is this a premonition or is this a truth?

Man: *What do you mean?*

Vianna: I mean, if you have all these things, is this really going to happen? Are you really going to be lonely?

Man: *I don't think so. It's just how I'm feeling.*

Vianna: Okay, so why do you feel that way?

Man: *It's the way I've always felt.*

Vianna: You've always felt lonely?

Man: *Yeah.*

Vianna: Always? Okay, so why do you feel lonely?

Man: *Because no matter what relationships I become involved in, I'm always alone when I'm living in them.*

Vianna: I noticed that you manifested two houses and traveling, but you never set up a relationship. That's kind of interesting.

Man: *Isn't it now?*

Vianna: So, no matter how your relationship is and no matter what your relationship is, you are always lonely. Say that.

Man: *No matter how my relationship is or what my relationship is, I am always lonely. [He energy tests 'yes.']*

Vianna: Okay, so why is that?

Man: *Because the people I've tried to connect with just aren't on the same page, or we're always going in different directions, or we don't want the same thing.*

Vianna: Do you know what it feels like to have a good relationship? Do you know how to create a good relationship?

Man: *I am guessing not, since I haven't.*

Vianna: So say: 'I attract people who are always going to pull me in the wrong direction.' [*He energy tests 'yes.'*] So, are these women the opposite of you?

Man: *No, just different.*

Vianna: So say: 'I know how to attract somebody like me.'

Man: *I know how to attract somebody like me. [He energy tests 'yes.']*

Vianna: So, what do you want in another person?

Man: *You know, I don't know. In some ways I know what I think I like, but it turns out that I never really know what I think I like.*

Vianna: So should we teach you that it is possible to know what you want?

Man: *Okay.*

Vianna: Let's teach you that it is possible to know what you want and that you know how to attract someone who is a compatible soul mate and will grow with you. Is that okay?

Man: *Okay.*

Vianna: Let's teach you that you are able to live your life without being lonely and that it is possible to do that. Okay. Now, you say you are different from other people. Does that mean you pull away from other people, or are you just so different that nobody understands you, or do you feel that it is it sacred to be alone?

Man: *Probably it's sacred to be alone.*

Vianna to class: He is doing that 'No women want me, I just don't want them' kind of thing. [*To man:*] Repeat after me: 'It is safe for me to be alone.'

Man: *It is safe for me to be alone. [He energy tests 'yes.']*

Vianna: Would you like to know what it feels like to be safe in your world?

Man: *Okay.*

Vianna to class: When I downloaded what it felt like to be safe in his world, he had a panicky look on his face. When you do a download, people are supposed to go 'Aaaah' and say, 'That feels great.' He doesn't look like he's happy with that download. [*To man:*] Okay, so it's safer to be alone. Why?

Man: *Because I'm not going to get hurt.*

Vianna: So you're not going to get hurt if you're alone? Why?

Man: *Why? Hmm, I don't know.*

Vianna: How long have you felt that way?

Man: *It feels like forever.*

Vianna: So you've felt this loneliness feeling 'forever,' because it's safe to be lonely. Say: 'It is safe to be lonely.'

Man: *It is safe to be lonely.* [He energy tests 'yes.']

Vianna: Okay, but that doesn't have to go on forever. Would you like to know what it feels like to be safe and share your life with somebody?

Man: *Yes.*

Vianna: Now, if somebody really knows you inside, what's the worst thing that could happen?

Man: *They could leave me.*

Vianna: So really, they're not just going to hurt you, they're going to leave you. So say, 'If they really know me, they are going to leave me.'

Man: *If they really know me, they are going to leave me.'*

Vianna: No, that's not the right program. Instead, say, 'If they really know my heart, they are going to leave me.'

Man: *If they really know my heart, they are going to leave me. [He energy tests 'yes.']*

Vianna: So how can you let someone love you? It's safer to be alone, because it's less complicated than if they leave you. Would you like to know what it feels like to have somebody stay? Or is it better if they leave you? Do you force them to leave you?

Man: *I don't think so.*

Vianna: Who left you?

Man: *Oh, not literally physically, but my mother kind of left me.*

Vianna: What does that mean to you?

Man: *I don't understand what you mean.*

Vianna: How did she leave you?

Man: *She left me by not acknowledging me. The form that this took began when I was a small child. If I wasn't giving her the answer that she wanted, there were times when she would literally go blank and stop receiving the conversation and just walk away, just like a five-year-old child would when they were angry. There were times when I couldn't make a connection with her at all. When I was a teenager, versions of the same thing would happen.*

Vianna: You are doing your best to make the relationship work, but they are still leaving you... Is this all women, or just your mother? Is this all the women you care about?

Man: *Yeah, pretty much, I guess.*

Vianna: So would you like to know how to connect with another person? How to be important? How to be treated with respect and love? Would you like to know that it is possible? Is that okay?

Man: *Yeah.*

Vianna: So how do you feel now?

Man: *Sad.*

Vianna: Is it a better sad or a lesser sad?

Man: *Uh, grieving sad.*

Vianna: You must have been a sad little boy who couldn't connect. Let's teach you that you can connect on a spiritual, physical and mental level with people, and that you can truly, completely connect with everyone around you, and that you can draw friends to you who uplift you and are loyal friends. Is that okay?

Man: *Yes.*

Vianna: And that you know what it feels like to be loyal to someone. And have them be loyal to you and have them connect with you, and that it is safe to do that. That you attract trustworthy people to you, and people who don't act like a five-year-old child with their emotions. Is that okay? [*To class:*] Don't get me wrong – acting like a child isn't always a bad thing and can sometimes be good. [*To man:*] How would you like to know how to deal with somebody who doesn't connect with you?

Man: *Well, yes, I would. Back then I had no idea – I was five years old when it happened…*

Vianna: Had it ever happened before?

Man: *Probably, but that was the moment when I realized how wrong it was and how it hurt.*

Vianna: Okay, so I need you to go back to the time when you were that five-year-old boy. Now I want you to see yourself as an adult standing there beside that little boy and I want you to reach over and give him a hug. Now close your eyes and manifest. Does the person you are in a relationship with understand you?

Man: *Yeah.*

Vianna: Do you understand her? Do you still like her?

Man: *So far.*

Vianna: Close your eyes. Does she travel with you?

Man: *Sometimes.*

Vianna: Is it better when she travels with you?

Man: *Sometimes.*

Vianna: Okay. Are you cool with this situation?

Man: *Yeah.*

Vianna: Does it feel more real, possible?

Man: *Yeah.*

Vianna: Okay, the friends who are in your life, are they still the friends you knew before, or are they new friends?

Man: *Some of them are the friends I have now.*

Vianna: Good thing! How do you feel?

Man: *I feel much better – happier. Things feel much more attainable. Yeah, it feels much more real.*

Vianna nods her head: Yes, it's much more real. [*To class:*] Okay, so we just worked on the two subjects of: 'What's the worst that could happen if you had this in your life?' and 'How are people going to feel about you if you have abundance?' His block on love had nothing to do with money or houses or traveling. What was his block? He didn't want to be alone in a big old house by himself. Because of this, he wasn't going to create a big old house. Now he has someone to share it with, he can have it. Let's check him for something else. [*To man:*] Repeat after me: 'I will be lonely.'

Man: *I will be lonely. If I manifest what I want, I will be lonely. [He energy tests 'no.']*

Vianna to class: Okay, what else would you test him for?

Student: *See if he knows how to create a good relationship.*

Vianna: Repeat after me: 'I know how to create a good relationship.'

Man: *I know how to create a good relationship. [He energy tests 'yes.']*

Vianna: So he knows how to create a good relationship. Repeat after me, 'I know how to draw someone compatible to me.'

Man: *I know how to draw someone compatible to me. [He energy tests 'yes.']*

Student: *Check him to find out if he believes anyone exists who is compatible with him.*

Vianna: Repeat after me: 'Someone exists who is compatible with me.'

Man: *Someone exists who is compatible with me.*

Vianna: Hold tight – tighter, tighter, tighter. Yes, he believes that there is someone out there. Okay then, let's check him for 'I am the prize.'

Man: *I am the prize. [He energy tests 'yes.']*

Vianna: Okay, say: 'I know how to connect to other people.'

Man: *I know how to connect to other people. [He energy tests 'yes.']*

Vianna: I know how to connect to a woman I care for.

Man: *I know how to connect to a woman I care for.*

Woman: If a woman sees my heart, she is going to run.

Man: *If a woman sees my heart, she is going to run. [He energy tests 'no.']*

Vianna to class: Does he need more belief work? Maybe, but this will make it possible for him to find both abundance and love, since they are the same thing.

Part II

THE
SOUL-MATE
QUEST

Chapter 5

PREPARING FOR A SOUL MATE

Many people are on a quest to find their soul mate. In some instances the quest becomes more important than accomplishing the goal. Be careful searching for your soul mate, because I have seen people who have become addicted to the search and they will always be looking for their soul mate.

As humanity is evolving, there are more soul mates to choose from now than ever before. We may have dozens of soul mates, in all shapes and sizes. We will also have more than one compatible soul mate. How can we make sure we draw the most compatible one to us?

TRUST IN THE DIVINE

You should work on your issues of trusting that the universe will bring you and your soul mate together. There is nothing wrong with searching for your soul mate, but when it becomes compulsive behavior, the *search* becomes the only goal and there is no completion. It is like a mystical quest for the Holy Grail that has no beginning and no end. It is the quest that is the focus and not the conclusion.

You can become so used to talking about how you don't have a soul mate that this is all that you will manifest. This is because you are telling your subconscious mind day in and day out, 'I can't find my soul mate' and 'There's no one out there for me' and are asking, 'Why haven't I found them yet, why have I been forgotten?' All these negative thoughts and words are preventing the universe from creating the circumstances in which you can meet that most important person in your life.

The question that many people ask is: 'Where is my soul mate?'

But for most people, this isn't what they should be asking. The questions they should be asking are:

- 'What is a soul mate?'

- 'What kind of person do I want to be with?'

- 'What do I have to offer this special person?'

- 'What will I do with my soul mate when I get them?'

LOVE THYSELF TO LOVE OTHERS

A soul mate can make you happy or tear you apart emotionally, depending on how you feel about yourself. If you haven't arrived at a point in time where you can truly love yourself, a soul-mate relationship will drag you over the coals.

As soon as you begin to love yourself, an interesting energy will arise in your heart chakra. This will trigger your sexual chakra to call for your compatible soul mate.

When you begin to call for your compatible soul mate, though, you will find that you draw other people to you too, people who are attracted to your pulsating energy. Not everyone who is attracted to you is going to be your soul mate, and not every soul mate is going to be compatible with you.

The best way to attract a compatible soul-mate is to love yourself and be proud of who you are. When you know and love yourself, you are ready for your *most compatible* soul mate. The level of development you have attained as a person is what will ultimately dictate the soul mate that you draw from the All That Is energy.

Many people believe that they cannot be complete until they find their soul mate, but the reverse is true. People must be complete in themselves first. To be truly compatible, both people must love themselves and, from this self-love, generate an inner happiness that blossoms outward. This is what makes the energies of soul mates truly compatible.

Many people *demand* to have their most compatible soul mate, but they aren't ready for them because of self-hate. You have to love yourself first.

'It's All About Me!'

Here's another scenario I see in clients and students: when someone finally finds a soul mate, it's all about *them* and not about the other person at all. This is hardly conducive to an equal and loving relationship. Both people should feel free to be open and share how they make a living, their likes and dislikes, and all the many facets of their personality in comfort and safety. They should feel free to share profound parts of themselves, otherwise the relationship will be built upon a façade. It will be based upon the wants and needs of one or the other of the parties and not both.

Think to yourself, what do you have to give back? What makes you the prize? What makes someone want to be with you?

If you can't think of anything, these are the areas that you need to work on. Your message to the universe should be: 'This is what I am looking for in another person and this is what I have to give back.'

Write down three things that you want in a person and three things that you will give back to them.

BE ALERT AND READY TO ACT

You can find soul mates all the time. Remember that you have more than one and you can always create a new one in this place and time.

Still, many of us are looking for something that is already on a deeper level. We are looking for a love that is deep and unquenchable, something that was with us before we came here and will be with us forever, a special someone to share our thoughts and feelings with, and *their* thoughts and feelings. We are looking for someone to walk with us through our life and beyond, something *everlasting*. This may be a little trickier.

When you ask psychic questions about a soul mate, it is important to be able to interpret the information you are told correctly and apply it in your life. Some people ask the divine energies, 'When will I meet my soul mate?' and are given a date and sometimes a time. The date and time pass and they are unaware that they have actually met their soul mate. This is because when they asked these questions, what they got were *possibilities* of when and how they *could* meet their soul mate. The divine can direct and guide us, but we have to stay alert and take the right actions to make things happen.

For instance, you might ask God when you are going to meet your soul mate and be told that you will meet him on December 22 and he will be wearing a red hat. December 22 comes and goes and you don't think you've met anybody in a red hat. But what you've missed is that on December 22 you went to a Christmas party and there was a man there playing Santa Claus and wearing a red hat! This person was your soul mate but you completely overlooked him. Four months later, it hits you: 'Oh my God, that was him!'

You were given the right information, but you didn't ask enough questions. If you ever feel unclear about what you are told, keep asking questions.

Also, be prepared to act on the information. I know of many people who were told by the divine that they should move from the place they were currently living in order to meet their most compatible soul mate. However, they refused to move, and guess what? They didn't meet their most compatible soul mate.

Are you ready to take the action needed to be with that special someone?

BE PATIENT

Ultimatums to God

A common theme with people who ask for their soul mate is to blame God when the soul mate doesn't immediately come into their lives. They become angry with God as if it is somehow God's fault, instead of perceiving that it is most likely down to their own shortcomings.

Another common mistake is to make demands of God and give ultimatums. People say, 'God, I *demand* [not request!] that I have my soul mate now.' Or they may not use that exact wording in their manifesting prayer, but they do have that energy, and it is the energy that is important when a manifestation is requested.

After doing thousands of readings, I found a common theme with regard to soul-mate timing. Let's take one particular instance.

A woman asks me, 'Where is my soul mate? I want him now!'

I tell her, 'Okay, I will go and take a peek at your future.'

When I go up to perceive her future, I see that her soul mate won't be ready for her yet.

So I tell her, 'At this time your soul mate is unstable. He won't be ready for another year at least. However, two years from now his life will become more stable and he will be really ready for a relationship.'

Disappointed, the woman says, 'Oh, but he has to be ready for me now!'

She ignores my advice and begins to compulsively bug God, demanding, 'I want him now! I want him now! I want him now!'

Several weeks later, God finally says, 'Okay!'

Is this what this woman really wants? No! Because of this *demand* she finds her soul mate, but it is far too early and he is a complete blithering idiot! However, this doesn't deter her, because this man is her true soul mate and she is irresistibly drawn to him.

So he comes into her life, but he is going through a divorce and it is obvious he is emotionally unstable. So she begins to blame God. She appeals to God, complaining, 'This is all wrong!'

The answer from God comes in as, 'Well, he wouldn't have been unstable if you hadn't brought him out of the oven too early. He had to cook for two years and if you had let him do that he would have been a beautiful cake that was ready for you.'

Because of the rush and impatience, the new couple spends the next year in unstable situations until finally things smooth out for them.

Should this woman have listened to the advice? Yes, but waiting is difficult in affairs of the heart, isn't it?

By giving this woman what she wanted, what was the Creator doing? To the Creator, it is all a learning process and learning from a difficult experience is the same as learning from an easy one. Ultimately, it is up to us if the experience is a difficult one or a good one. We always have free will.

Any time that people give ultimatums to God, it is likely that they have some kind of lack in their personality. In a general sense, they have a real fear that their prayers might actually be answered, and once they are, it is all God's fault and not their own.

CHECK YOUR BELIEFS

We have already looked at working on your beliefs. People are drawn to one another because of the negative beliefs they share as well as the positive beliefs. So you should remove as many negative beliefs as possible and do feeling work on yourself to attract the best person you can.

One area where your beliefs may be holding you back from finding your soul mate is physical sickness.

The Soul Mate and Sickness

Some people are attached to their physical sickness because on a deep level they fear change and personal growth. In some instances people will be so attached to their sickness that they won't draw their soul mate to them, because this represents a major life-changing event. In this scenario, the person will remain sick and won't take the steps to get better.

It's possible that if you believe you will be hurt if you are happy, your brain will keep you sick. You might have the program of 'If I am happy and fall in love, they will leave me or hurt me.' So you may draw someone who isn't a compatible soul mate.

Your brain loves you enough to run this program for you. So in many instances it is finding out how the sickness is serving you that is important. If you can clear this energy, you can understand that you can be happy without fearing change and can therefore find your soul mate.

Ask yourself what would happen if you found your soul mate. You might be happy and full of joy. Ask yourself what would happen if you were happy and full of joy. What would happen?

BE POSITIVE

There is someone out there for all of us. When someone tells me that there is no one out there for them, I tell them to go to a supermarket and 'people watch' for a while. They will see lots of couples, and some of them resemble human beings, but some do not! If these people can find someone, then anyone can!

If you tell the universe that there's no one out there, then no one is what you will manifest. And what you really want to manifest is positive people.

MANIFESTING POSITIVE PEOPLE

1. Center yourself in your heart and visualize going down into Mother Earth, which is a part of All That Is.

2. Go up through your crown chakra in a ball of light and project your consciousness out past the stars to the universe.

3. Go beyond the universe, past the layers of light, through the golden light, past the jelly-like substance that is the Laws, into a pearly, iridescent white light, the Seventh Plane of Existence.

4. Make the command to your subconscious and request to the Creator:

    'Creator of All That Is, it is commanded that I bring people to me who are like-minded. Thank you! It is done, it is done, it is done.'

5. Witness like-minded people coming into your life in the future.

6. As soon as the process is finished, rinse yourself off with Seventh-Plane energy and stay connected to it.

In the following chapter I will show you how to manifest a soul mate. When you do this, always ask for your *most compatible soul mate* in the *highest and best way* when you send your message out to the universe through the Creator of All That Is. That way you have a much better chance of finding one who is attuned to you mentally, sexually, spiritually, physically, and emotionally.

However, the highest and best way doesn't always mean that it is the easiest. There may be some interesting times ahead on your soul-mate quest...

Chapter 6

MANIFESTING A SOUL MATE

If you are going to manifest a soul mate, first of all you have to be sure that's really what you want. Are you ready to share your life with someone? Ask your heart if you are really ready to share everything with another person. Are you looking for a soul mate or a slave?

What is the worst thing that can happen if you get what you want? Is there a voice inside you that tells you that you don't deserve it or makes you worry about what will happen once you get it? Work on this voice, on the beliefs that give it the power to speak.

If you ask the Creator to take you to where you should be to meet your soul mate, are you sure you're ready to move to that place?

If you get a soul mate, are you ready to spend time with them? If you get bored with only one partner, maybe it's because you don't have the gene for monogamy (not everyone carries this; *see Chapter 10*).

All these things come into play when you are manifesting a soul mate. So, even though you may feel you're fully prepared, ask yourself the following questions:

- Do you want a soul mate now or do you want a companion now?

- Do you have something to offer someone else?

- What makes you the prize?

- What do you know about the opposite sex?

- Are you willing to learn and always keep learning?

- Do you know that you deserve to fulfil your dreams?

KNOW WHAT YOU WANT

Once you're sure you're ready to manifest a soul mate, you have to know exactly what you want. When you go up and ask God for a soul mate, you have to be very specific. You have to be precise about the gender, even the species, because if you ask for somebody who loves you unconditionally, you might receive a dog.

- Do you want a rich soul mate?

- Do you want them to be single or married?

- Do you want them to share their fortune with you?

Many people will sit down and write a long list of what they want in another person. I know people who've written down everything they can think of, but forgotten the most important thing: that their soul mate is compatible with them and they are in love.

Don't ask for a *perfect* soul mate, since they may be *too* perfect. Instead, ask for your *most compatible* soul mate.

If you have a preference as to whether or not someone is faithful sexually, specify that your soul mate has the monogamy gene.

The following exercise will help you to clarify what you want and, importantly, what you have to offer in return:

KNOW WHAT YOU WANT IN A SOUL MATE

1. List four traits that you wish for in a soul mate.

2. As someone else what they think is important and borrow two of the traits they come up with.

3. Write the four best qualities that you have to offer your soul mate.

4. List two qualities that others see in you.

5. List all the qualities that your soul mate will have.

MANIFESTING

Here are several ways to manifest your soul mate:

CALLING FOR YOUR COMPATIBLE SOUL MATE

1. Center yourself in your heart and visualize going down into Mother Earth, which is a part of All That Is.

2. Go up through your crown chakra in a ball of light and project your consciousness out past the stars to the universe.

3. Go beyond the universe, past the layers of light, through the golden light, past the jelly-like substance that is the Laws, into a pearly, iridescent white light, the Seventh Plane of Existence.

4. Make the command to your subconscious and request to the Creator:

> 'Creator of All That Is, it is commanded that my
> most compatible life soul mate be brought to me,
> and that they have these attributes [state attributes].
> Thank you! It is done, it is done, it is done.'

5. Witness the call to your most compatible soul mate being sent out.

6. As soon as the process is finished, rinse yourself off with Seventh-Plane energy and stay connected to it.

Note the following:

- If you command that you have your most compatible soul mate *now*, you will pull in whoever is the most compatible person right now. This may not be the most compatible one of all.

- If you want someone to spend your life with, instead of saying that you want a compatible soul mate, ask for your most compatible *divine life soul mate*.

MANIFESTATION FOR 10 DAYS

1. Take your list of all the things you want your soul mate to be and put it by your bed.

2. Go up to the Seventh Plane as before. Imagine that person while in the theta state.

3. Do this every day for at least 10 days.

4. Each morning, meditate on being the person *you* want to be in your soul-mate relationship.

PYRAMID EXERCISE TO FIND YOUR SOUL MATE

One of the most important exercises for calling in your soul mate is the following meditation. I have used it throughout my life to bring in abundance of all kinds.

In this exercise we are using pyramid energy to magnify the manifestation.

1. Go up to the Seventh Plane as before.

2. Make the command:

> *'Creator of All That Is, it is commanded that I bring my compatible soul-mate into my life. Thank you! It is done. It is done, it is done.'*

3. Witness yourself standing under a huge pyramid. Witness the energy of your request being sent up into the center of the pyramid to be magnified and sent to the universe.

4. As soon as the process is finished, rinse yourself off with Seventh-Plane energy and stay connected to it.

Chapter 7

DATING ADVICE
FOR SOUL MATES

In this chapter we will discuss some practical aspects that can help in finding a soul mate. To some, this information may seem redundant, but I was surprised at how many of my clients and students were naïve to the simple nuances of relationships.

IT'S RAINING SOUL MATES!

It's likely that once you begin to call for a soul mate you will bring in more than one *at the same time*. This is because you will be giving a signal out to the universe that you really love yourself and that you are ready for a soul mate.

Whatever you want, however difficult, be prepared for it to come your way. I remember one particular woman who came into my shop and said in the snootiest way possible, 'I want my soul mate! I want him to be a manly man, but I don't want him to watch sports, I want him to wait on me hand and foot, take care of me and rub my feet! I want him to go shopping with me and know all the different shoe fashions!'

I thought to myself, We live in Idaho, where the men are men! They like hunting, fishing, sports, and women – generally in that order. A manly man is relatively easy to find. One who likes to shop for things that women like and knows the styles of shoes in Italy – well, that might be pushing the manifestation a little too far.

So I said to the woman, 'Are you sure that you want a manly man? Wouldn't you rather have a gay friend to do things with?'

She told me, 'No, I want my soul mate!'

So here she is, making all these demands on the universe and on the free will of another person, and not once understanding that she has to give as well as receive in a relationship. The give and take in any relationship should start at the spiritual level.

I don't know what happened to her, but I do know that I was telling this story in one of my classes when one woman told the class, 'I found my soul mate, and he does know all the shoe fashions, enjoys shopping with me, and is still a manly man!'

Apparently he was an understanding heterosexual man from California.

DATING

Once you have met someone and they want to go out on a date with you, what then? There are some people who need to be coached on how to date. And there are those who *date* and those who *marry*. Which one are you? Are you the marrying type? Do you want to spend your life with another person in a monogamous relationship? If this is what you want, then this is what you should manifest into reality, not a series of dates. Otherwise, you are only fooling yourself.

Blind dates in particular are not very successful in accomplishing this goal. There are better ways of finding your soul mate and it is very important that you know exactly what you want so that you don't send confusing requests to the universe.

AFFIRMATIONS FOR SOUL MATES

To bring the right date to you, you might like to try the following affirmations. An affirmation is a declaration to your unconscious mind as well as to the universe of what you expect of it.

For 10 days, read these affirmations each night before you go to sleep:

'Every day, in every way, I get better.'

*'In every way I am allowing the universe to
bring me my compatible soul mate.'*

'My compatible soul mate is in my life with the right timing.'

'I just get better and better.'

'I will honor this love.'

'I deserve this love.'

'I am the prize.'

Online Dating

The internet has brought us better communication than ever before. All over the world people are talking to one another and many meet online through dating sites. At first, this may seem like a good idea, and some people do find their true love online. However, online dating presents its own problems.

The thing is, online, people don't have to be who they really are. There is an element of illusion there. Predators use this in the way that they present themselves. Married people use it to start affairs.

When you finally meet someone you've got to know online, they may not even be close to how they presented themselves. Some people even present themselves as a different sexual orientation.

When setting up a meeting, precautions for your personal safety are a must. The world is full of all kinds of people and some of them aren't exactly nice. If you meet someone online and then decide to meet them in the flesh, do so in a public place and take a friend with you.

Early Stages

However people meet, both parties must agree that they are indeed compatible soul mates for a relationship to start, and it may not be immediately evident that they are soul mates at all. One person may realize that they have found true love before the other.

If you are this person, it is important that you don't frighten your soul mate off by being over-exuberant toward them. It may take a little time for both people to realize what's happening. This will mostly be because of the fears that have been generated by past relationships.

I have also observed that many people use the soul-mate concept as a come-on when they first meet. They claim they knew the person in a past life and tell them so. This come-on has become almost as pervading as 'What's your zodiac sign?', at least in some spiritual circles.

There are few things more unsettling than to have someone you've just met tell you that they knew you in a past life and they are your soul mate.

DATING AND SEX

When you meet a person and have feelings for them, you should find out if these are deep and meaningful or just based on physical attraction. Physical attraction is a very strong instinct, but should not be confused with the feelings we have for a real soul mate. Although you will be sexually attracted to your divine mate, you should know the difference between hormones and spirituality.

(However, having said this, I have heard of people having a Platonic relationship with their soul mate and being happy with this arrangement.)

Most people do not teach proper dating practices to their children, and it certainly isn't taught in school either. Another thing that isn't taught to most children is how sex is spiritually tied to who we are. I feel that children should understand that when they have sex, there is an energy exchange that can last for seven years as an imprint in their physical and etheric bodies.

This is why it is important to go on a date with someone who is compatible with you. Do not 'mercy date' and do not engage in 'sport dating.' These practices are not conducive to spiritual growth.

Furthermore, scientists recently made the discovery that people who have sex are leaving their DNA behind in each other's bodies. At our present level of technology, it is difficult to say how much of this 'DNA exchange' is beneficial, but as it relates to the transference of disease, it definitely is not.

For instance, doctors have recently discovered traces of the DNA of the Ebola virus in the sperm of a man who recovered from the disease during a recent outbreak in Africa. He tested positive for traces of Ebola DNA for three months before they were finally gone. This is because the reproductive system is insulated from the rest of the body and viruses and bacteria can last longer in this protected zone. They can be in the reproductive system without being in the bloodstream.

Ladies, You Are the Prize

One of my clients told me she couldn't figure out why men left her after they had visited her bedroom. Ladies, you should not have sex with a man too soon in a relationship. You have to think of yourself as the prize, the cherished gift, not the trophy. It is a mistake to look at an attractive person and think they are the prize! Well, okay, that is fine as long as you value yourself as much as you do them. But what makes *you* the prize? What makes you the catch?

Remember, you are the prize, and sex is just the frosting on the cake, so don't be frosting everything! The more energy that you spend on carrots (people who are not your soul mate), the less there is to send out for your soul mate.

Before you have sex with a person, make sure that it is someone that you want to be with. Investigate a person before you go too far into the relationship. There should be no guilt associated with investigating a prospective mate.

THE MALE AND FEMALE BRAIN

One point to bear in mind when dating is that men and women are different in the way that they use their brain. There has been a great deal of talk about the right-brain, left-brain theory. It is said that men are left-brained and women are right-brained. How does this affect their interaction?

If we go back to the womb, in the fourth month a baby boy experiences a flush of testosterone through his little body that is likely to make him more left-brained. This left-brain emphasis helps him to keep focused on one thing at a time, so he will be a good hunter, warrior, and protector. This is an age-old criterion of evolutionary development. But by the 1970s more and more boys were being born with right-brain attributes. Right-brain energy gives us the ability to empathize well with others and to multi-task on many levels.

Everyone is born with a certain tendency toward more right-brain or left-brain activity. If a woman is more left-brain oriented, she will have a tendency to get along very well with men. However, she may not get along very well with other women, because she can't figure them out, whereas a right-brained man can easily work with women.

In any pair-bond, heterosexual or homosexual, this right-brain, left-brain aspect will manifest in the relationship. One person or the other, regardless of gender, will take on the male role, and the other person will take on the female role.

In my relationship with my husband, our roles are sometimes unconventionally reversed. Because I teach in front of groups of people, I essentially take on more of the 'male role' in our relationship, and if my husband wasn't secure in his manliness, our relationship would be much more difficult.

In order to adapt to our unconventional relationship, both of us have changed our beliefs along with our roles. When Guy begins to tell me something about his day, I take on the male role and immediately attempt to fix it, without coming to the understanding that Guy does not want to fix it, he only wants to talk about it, much as a woman might. I am trying to fix it because I take on responsibilities every day, and this mentality washes over into our more intimate relationship. We don't always switch roles like this, though. Sometimes we are very conventional in our interaction with one another.

An interesting point with regard to male–female interaction is that many people say that men cannot get in touch with their feelings. I have found that men have deep feelings, but it is the way that they express them that makes them different from women. I have known men to lie down and die directly after their wife of 50 years has died. They just don't seem to be able to make the adjustment like a woman can. After the death of a spouse, most women are able to move on and get married again within a few years and live for another 20.

While there are many differences between the sexes, it is these differences that can enhance our relationship with our soul mate, if we can only understand them better. The key is to train the brain to be better balanced, so that right brain and left brain work together.

MALE–FEMALE BRAIN BALANCING

1. Center yourself in your heart and visualize going down into Mother Earth, which is a part of All That Is.

2. Go up through your crown chakra in a ball of light and project your consciousness out past the stars to the universe.

3. Go beyond the universe, past the layers of light, through the golden light, past the jelly-like substance that is the Laws, into a pearly, iridescent white light, the Seventh Plane of Existence.

4. Make the command to your subconscious and request to the Creator:

> 'Creator of All That Is, it is commanded that the male –
> female aspects of [person]'s brain be balanced in
> the highest and best way, as is appropriate at this
> time. Thank you! It is done, it is done, it is done.'

5. Move your consciousness over to the person's space. Go into their brain and witness the male and female aspects becoming balanced in the most appropriate way for them.

6. As soon as the process is finished, rinse yourself off with Seventh-Plane energy and stay connected to it.

SEND LOVE TO BABY IN THE WOMB

This exercise is for both men and women. Many people who have used ThetaHealing before will have already used it, so this is for those who haven't experienced it yet.

The reason that I use this exercise in relation to soul mates is because some people are confused about the kind of love that they want in a soul-mate relationship. If they don't understand what it feels like to be cherished, nurtured, and loved by their father and their mother, they may attempt to create this kind of love in a relationship with a lover. Some people do say that women will seek their father in their first relationship and men will seek their mother.

I once met a beautiful woman who felt that her husband was her father, friend, and husband all at the same time. To her, he filled the role of her father because she had never loved her father. This made him uncomfortable, though, because he didn't want to fill that role. This kind of relationship can be confusing.

We may never have felt the right kind of love and not know it. And as well as affecting our relationships, being loved from the beginning of our life can also play an important role in our overall health as we get older.

It is important that you know what it feels like to be loved by your parents from the time of conception. How were you conceived? What kind of situations were going on at the time? When your mother and father found out about the pregnancy, how did they feel? Were you wanted or not wanted? Were you given over for adoption? Was one of your siblings loved more than you were?

Some of you may have been born when people weren't using contraceptives as they do now. Was your mother happy when you were born or was she overwhelmed? What was the reception that you received when you were born?

From the moment of conception, we are aware of everything around us, including our mother's feelings, emotions, and beliefs. Feelings of being overwhelmed, of not wanting a child, and other stresses can all be passed on to us and affect our noradrenaline and serotonin levels. Some of us also start out as one of twins. Nature may only allow about one third of the twins that are conceived to survive. This sometimes produces loneliness in the remaining twin. Attempted abortions can also affect an individual.

The ancient Hawaiians considered it wrong for there to be arguments and discord around a woman who was pregnant. If this happened, the couple could face punishment after the birth of the child. It was believed that in order for the baby to have the best chance of survival, it needed to be surrounded with good energy and good vibrations from the point of conception.

What were your parents talking about when you were born? Was there excitement and welcoming energy or did they fight? Did they love the fact that you were coming? When you arrived, was it warm? Were you taken away from your mother? Were you breastfed?

All these memories have been kept inside your body. Like a sponge, you absorbed every word that was said. What words made you feel inadequate, not worthy, guilty, wonderful, proud of yourself? To release any negative energies from that time and understand what it is to be loved, you can send love to the baby in the womb.

SEND LOVE TO THE BABY IN THE WOMB

1. Center yourself in your heart and visualize going down into Mother Earth, which is a part of All That Is.

2. Go up through your crown chakra in a ball of light and project your consciousness out past the stars to the universe.

3. Go beyond the universe, past the layers of light, through the golden light, past the jelly-like substance that is the Laws, into a pearly, iridescent white light, the Seventh Plane of Existence.

4. Gather unconditional love and make the command:

    'Creator of All That Is, it is commanded that love, nurturing, compassion, and acceptance be sent to [yourself or another person] as a baby in the womb. Thank you. It is done, it is done, it is done.'

5. Now go up and witness the Creator's unconditional love surrounding the baby, whether it is you, your own child, or your parents. Witness love filling the womb and watch it envelop the fetus and eliminate all poisons, toxins, and negative emotions, surrounding the person with love from the beginning of their life, through their whole life, and beyond.

6. When you have finished, rinse yourself off in Seventh-Plane energy and stay connected to it.

Chapter 8

ADVICE FOR WOMEN

Girls, if you are interested, I will tell you what men want … they want you to be kind, sweet, wonderful, loving, and fun. You should be someone to do fun things with and tell *almost* everything to. And when it comes to that special time, men want you to be a really nice girl until you are in the bedroom. Then they would prefer a little bit of passion.

What do *you* want? A lot of women have an image of the kind of man they want. It's often a man who is brave and handsome, smart, rich, kind, loving, and accepting, with a strong masculine energy and the right amount of muscle. Okay, ladies, if he has muscles, it takes something to make them in the first place, and this means the man is involved in several things: sports, exercise, and outdoor endeavors!

There is a recurring theme with a lot of women I talk to about finding a soul mate: they want a 'manly man,' but as soon as they get him, they want to un-man him! Or they don't want to put in the effort to get him in the first place, especially if it means making changes to their own lives. They want to be with a manly man, but they also want to stay at home and watch TV, or go shopping.

What do you know about men? If you are attracted to them, it is important that you develop your knowledge of them so you can be in a relationship with one.

I once worked in male-oriented jobs and found that men can sometimes be foul, disgusting creatures when it comes to their animalistic tendencies and attitudes toward women. It goes without saying, but must be said: in the workplace, do not sleep around and you will maintain the respect of your male colleagues. Then you can have good friendships with them.

It was helpful to me that I could do most of the things that the men could (shoot guns and spar). I could shoot firearms better than most of them and I could hunt just as well. In this way, I developed the kind of friendships with men that most women do not have. These associations gave me the insights I needed to manifest the kind of man that I wanted.

When I got a divorce, I sat down and reflected on my situation. I thought about the kind of person I was and looked at the grade of man that I wanted to attract. I wanted to be with someone who was going to share his life with me. I wanted an outdoorsy kind of person who was physically strong but also romantic, devoted, monogamous, and poetic, and I got everything I wanted in Guy.

I knew that I couldn't be with an outdoor person if I was so prissy as to be useless in an outdoor situation. So I learned how to do outdoor things to make myself ready for the kind of person that I wanted to attract.

I also knew that I didn't want to be needy. 'Clingy,' needy energy is what pushes people away. I wanted to be attractive enough to the person I wanted for them to pursue me. I didn't want to be the one doing the chasing. This was the best decision that I ever made, because the courtship ritual of the chase is the natural thing between man and woman, and it is 'man-hunt-woman.' If the woman hunts the man, the man is confused and runs away. For it to work, he has to be intrigued enough to pursue the woman. This realization helped me create something remarkable.

When I started teaching classes, I watched women sit in their little world and profess what they wanted in a man while never making the effort to find him. If they did make any effort at all, they would go to a bar. Now, this isn't to say that there aren't good people in bars, but there are also a lot of what I call 'bottom feeders.' If you want to go fishing for the opposite sex, a bar is the wrong kind of bait and generally draws the wrong kind of fish!

On the other end of the dating location spectrum, women should know that there are men out there who will say anything for sex. I once had a client tell me that if he wanted to have sex, he would go to a church dance. He said, 'I promise them that I love God and occasionally I promise to marry them and I can usually get a woman that night.' Other clients have told me that they go to the grocery store to pick up lonely housewives because there is no commitment there.

Girls, don't date anyone unless you plan on marrying them or at least have an idea that you might want to be with them in a relationship. If you look at them and you wouldn't want to be with them, don't date them! Don't do any charity dates.

The reason that I say this is because some women have a tendency to become entangled in relationships for all the wrong reasons. This will only slow down the process of finding your soul mate.

Don't give in too easily and have sex with someone, either. Men like women who are easily bedded, but they don't take them home to their mother. If you want a man to love and respect you, don't give away the prize immediately. A man respects a woman who makes it difficult for him. Understand that hormones run men so much that they only seem to want one thing. It is your responsibility to tell them *no* in a nice way. Being too easy will only hurt your reputation, and your reputation is very important.

If you are sexually attracted to another person, it may be because of an exchange of pheromones. These are chemicals secreted by individuals that trigger a social reaction in members of the same species. There are many types of pheromone, producing a broad range of actions and reactions. For the purpose of our discussion we will call them messages that are sent between two people via the chemistry of the body.

This doesn't mean that the whole attraction thing is based upon smells that are emitted by the body. Both women and men are psychologically and physiologically hardwired to reject the alluring smells of another person, for various reasons. In humans, chemistry goes well beyond the animal attraction between men and women.

Ladies, there are certain things that indicate that the two of you have chemistry. But don't get carried away. Just because someone asks you out on a date doesn't mean that they want to take you home to their mother and marry you.

For instance, let's say that a person asks you out for a date. You meet up and become attracted to them, but after the date, they don't call you back for another date. In general terms this means that they are not interested in you. Do *not* attempt to call them back. Control yourself and go on with your life as if you are unconcerned. Calling a person back on a daily basis is called desperation or stalking, take your pick. When there is true chemistry, things will happen naturally between you, and they will feel compelled to call you and meet with you again.

SENDING THE RIGHT SIGNALS

Your soul mate will find you if you send out the right signals to the universe:

- Brush your teeth and practice good personal hygiene.

- Wear moderate clothing that is suggestive of your figure but not overly revealing.

- Wear a moonstone. It can help to bring your soul mate to you, encourage lucid dreaming, enhance psychic abilities, and calm emotions.

- Select a certain fragrance and wear it every time that you go out. This is so the fragrance stands out in your date's mind and then, when the date is over and they smell that fragrance again, they think of you. Quite frankly, if more women wore perfume and had good overall hygiene, they would get asked out more often.

- Avoid talking too much about your other relationships. Rather, concentrate upon learning about the other person. Let them speak freely about themselves without interrogating them, as this is humiliating.

- It is a bad idea to tell them that you think they are your soul mate and you want to marry them.

- Find out what they are interested in. Find out what they like and be a little flexible. If you can come to enjoy some of the same things, you will have a better chance of having a shared relationship. One of the things that interests a man is a woman who is willing to share 'manly' pursuits and vice versa. This is a selling point to make you more appealing to the opposite sex. Many people expect their soul mate to fall in love with them completely and wait on them hand and foot, but in reality it is useful to have an interest in what the other person likes. Relationships are not all about you.

- Put yourself in a position where you are available to be seen by the type of person you want to attract. If your whole world is centered on doing things with other women, it will be difficult to attract a man. Community events are good places to meet people. If your career is not conducive to meeting people, do something extracurricular! However, you are not 'hunting' a person, you are 'drawing' someone to you. If you choose to go out on the town, remember, alcohol always creates a weakness in morals. Avoid drinking too much alcohol so that you can make good decisions.

- It is important to develop your self-esteem. You must have faith and know that your soul mate is coming, but at the same time you need to know that you will be fine without them.

- Many women believe that handsome men are shallow. This is an untruth and is generally only in the mind of the woman.

- It is hard for men to ask women out on dates. Some men get their feelings hurt very easily if they are rejected. However, you must allow a man to pursue you. If he is truly interested, he will pursue you.

- If you are in a budding relationship, do your best not to say anything bad about the person's mother. Even if they say something bad about their mother, don't play into it.

- Avoid coming on to married men. Everyone deserves to be number one in their partner's life.

- Don't try to change a man too much. Women often attempt to make men what they want them to be instead of what they are. This is always room for growth, but change may be unrealistic in some individuals.

THE CREATOR'S DEFINITIONS

In modern society many women think that they are 'as good as a man.' To this kind of thinking, I say several things. If a woman can do the same job as a man and do it as well, she should be paid the same and have the same chance of advancement. But when it comes to soul mates, this is not the issue. Somewhere in the sexual revolution we have forgotten that we are women. We have forgotten the power of being a woman. The goddess energy is within every woman and I think that it is time to celebrate what we are and the powers that we have – compassion, kindness, and the ability to raise a child and be a mother. There is also the ability to love and care for our spouses as no one else can – with a woman's touch. Every woman should know God's definition of a woman, and should be one, not only in the workplace but at home as well.

It is the same with a man. In this changing world where people are attempting to define what a man should and should not be, maybe we should know what the Creator's definition of what a man is. According to the Creator's definition, a man is strong, protective of those he loves, caring, and decisive.

In every relationship, the partners will assume male and female roles. Male and female are co-partners in a soul-mate relationship. This means that they work together, using the skills that God gave them and cultivating those that need to be awakened.

Chapter 9

ADVICE FOR MEN

Men, ask yourself, do you want a woman who wears high heels and beautiful clothes? Do you want a woman who just looks good on your arm or do you want a woman who can share everything with you? Do you want to find someone who shares your interests in the outdoors? If so, golf and racquetball are good compromise choices.

If you want to meet nice women, go to a metaphysical seminar! At the ThetaHealing Institute we had to plant trees so that the men who were driving by didn't slow down to stare at the women who were sitting on the lawn doing belief work. Several local men actually stopped in the middle of the road to stare at some of the Italian women who came to the institute. You have no idea how many men take our classes just to meet women. The ironic thing is that the women who come to the institute go off to play golf because that's where they think the men are!

But gentlemen, if you're just looking for sex, close this book. The subject matter of this book is not 'sport dating' and it will not help you in this way. It is about growing emotionally so that you can have a decent, lasting relationship. Know who you are, what you want, and work on what you can improve on. Sex will be there if you are patient.

To be in a relationship with a woman, it is important to develop a decent knowledge of women – or at least a basic understanding of the female psyche. This will help you understand the needs of women.

In modern times women have become increasingly empowered in all aspects of society. All the control that was once imposed upon them is falling away, at least in developed countries. Because of this, they now have different expectations of men. They used to want a man to support them, but this is no longer so prevalent. Now they expect men to be more sensitive, yet still be men. Some men feel that this is an unrealistic goal. In general, men need to find a compromise between the sensitivity that fulfills a woman's needs and their own masculinity.

Some women are more traditional, however. They want a man to be handsome, strong, and secure in himself and his finances. If this is the kind of woman you want, then you will have to be able to materially fill this role to attract her.

But there are women out there who are willing to build something together with a man, provided they are put first in his life. This aspect of a relationship is key to any woman. If a woman feels that she is the most important thing in your life, then your relationship will be much smoother. However, if you make your male friends more important, there can be issues between the two of you. This is also true if your mother is perceived to be more important than the woman in your life.

SENDING THE RIGHT SIGNALS

Your soul mate will find you if you send out the right signals to the universe. I once did a reading for a man who had lived alone his whole life. I saw that he was going to meet his soul mate and I told him so. He was dubious and told me that he had lived alone for too many years and didn't think that things would ever change and he was too old to fall in love. This is the wrong kind of message to send to the universe.

One day this man took his dog for a walk. The dog led him to another dog, which was walking along the same path. There on the other end of the leash was the love of his life. She had never been in love and never been married. They fell in love and acted like 20-year-old kids.

So, be prepared and send out the right signals:

- Good personal hygiene is all-important and you should dress the best that you can. Deodorant and clean teeth and nails are a very good idea.

- Be confident but not overbearing.

- Many men believe that beautiful women are shallow. This is an untruth and is generally only in the mind of the man.

- It is important that you are persistent in your endeavor of pursuing a woman without stalking or acting desperate.

- Learn how to be romantic. Women like romance. Keep it going once you are together. Men are generally able to be romantic until they have 'captured' the woman and then they don't put any more effort in.

- Go on a trip together before you make a commitment. This is one of the best ways of finding out if you are compatible. You need a woman who is not only a friend and a lover, but also someone you can stand to be around.

- Kindness is all-important to a woman. At the same time, if you are a complete pushover, women will take advantage of you and not respect you.

- It is true that many women have money as the top priority, but there are some who have spirituality first. Second on the list is generally that the man is handsome. The third, at least with most women, is sex. This is why it is important to learn to be a good sexual partner. You should know how to satisfy a woman.

JUST ONE MORE WORD...

Men, you have to understand that most women love to talk. They love to talk about their old relationships so that they can work through any old issues they may have. They also love to share intimate details about their life because they want to feel that they can trust you.

When men begin to share their intimate feelings, it is possible that fear may come into the relationship. Men can be fearful of revealing too much about themselves.

As soon as one or the other person begins to feel as though they have shared too much, the vulnerable party may withdraw. This is why you have to clear your fears about being in an intimate relationship, or all you will attract will be other people who are fearful of relationships.

Chapter 10

THE SOUL MATE
AND SEX

In order to attract a man or a woman, you first have to know how it is done in practical terms. Much of this is about sex, and don't let anyone tell you different. Sex is a very powerful facet in the world of interaction between men and women.

I'm not talking about the act of sex itself, but the energy that is created when there is an attraction to another person. When this happens, the body begins to emit pheromones and hormones that course through the body. These chemical messengers send information inside the body as well as outside to the other person.

HORMONES

It is our hormones that give us the drive for sex. If you don't have enough dopamine, serotonin, estrogen, or testosterone in your system, you're not going to have a sex drive or enjoy sex, but there are many other benefits to these hormones, too. The hormones that give us the desire for sex also help us to enjoy listening to music. They also enhance our spirituality, when we pray to God. So, if the desire for sex isn't there, many other desires are likely to be lacking as well.

Testosterone and estrogen actually hold the two parts of our species together. In the past, the men were always the providers and the women took care of the children. Much of this instinctual drive comes from these hormones. This has obvious benefits and we probably wouldn't have survived as a species without the pair bond. As we can see, the union of souls has practical as well as romantic aspects to it.

We can see hormones materialistically as substances in our bodies, or we can perceive them as gifts from God. These marvelous substances not only bind us together for the survival of the species, but also act as spiritual energies on this plane of existence.

Another survival mechanism is the releasing of pheromones. In animalistic terms, I believe that our physical body is going to give off pheromones when we're attracted to a person who is 'compatible,' at least in some ways. We're releasing these pheromone 'scents' all the time on a physical level and I think that the soul does much the same thing with vibrations when searching for a soul mate.

People are drawn to one another by energy, and this energy is expressed in many ways. For instance, people are drawn to one another because of how they look and how they act. They are drawn to compatible pheromones and also because they can sense that their own hormones are working correctly on the other person. If we emit confusing smells to one another, it is difficult for us to tell if a person is attracted to us. The proper balance of hormones in the body will enable us to act a certain way toward others. With this balance, we can give off the right signals to the opposite sex.

The Complete System of Self-Healing: Internal Exercises by Stephen Chang is an excellent book for balancing the hormones through Taoist exercises. In this book there are many internal exercises, one of which is the deer exercise. This helps to balance hormones in both women and men with or without having sex. It claims that it can make breasts larger or smaller, depending on what you want. It also gives men more staying power and can help get rid of any lumps and cysts. It tightens the woman to allow her to respond to sex, and also massages the internal organs and gives more energy.

Because of our diet, we often don't get the vitamins and minerals needed to create the ongoing supply of hormones that keeps our testosterone and estrogen levels balanced. In some instances, people do not get enough lipids to create hormones. There are, however, natural hormone replacements available.

Low testosterone and low estrogen have become widespread problems in industrial areas of the world for various reasons. Diet, birth control, caffeine use, drug and alcohol abuse, pharmaceutical drugs, injuries, and heavy metal poisoning are just a few of the causes of hormonal imbalances and infertility. It is only recently that prescription testosterone applied without injection has been made available to men and women with low levels of the hormone.

Men with low testosterone will have low energy and bone loss, become flabby and experience erectile dysfunction. If the cause is high blood pressure or heart disease, then the low testosterone is a domino effect of these disorders. But if the low testosterone has been caused by an injury, then the loss of adequate bioavailable testosterone can *cause* high blood pressure and heart disease. This shows us just how interrelated all the body's functions are.

Without estrogen, you cannot live. Estrogen is the key component that meets with serotonin in the brain and helps with memory.

In both men and women, the hormones are the best way of knowing if there is too much stress in your life. For instance, wrinkles in the skin can be delayed by maintaining proper hormone levels. If you have hormone imbalances, emotional stress may be the cause. This is where belief work can save the day!

Other things that help are selenium and zinc. Zinc is the needed for testosterone. You also have to have zinc in order to help vitamin C work in the body. Lecithin is an aid to the sexual functions. If you have had really bad bronchitis there is a good chance that your body never recovered; this can also cause hormonal disturbances. A lot of people will develop asthma because of the bronchitis, and zinc can help them make a full recovery. Another supplement that may help is edible bentonite clay.

Suggested Magic Potion for Impotency

If the person has no sexual appetite and the cause isn't emotional or psychological, then there could be a shortage of vitamins. For increasing the sex drive:

- Selenium, lecithin, as directed by your doctor, vitamin E, as directed, Damiana as directed. Do not suggest Damiana if the person has or has had prostate cancer or any sexual cancer. This is because it has estrogen in it and some compounds that may stimulate cancer. But all the others can be used to enhance sexual drive.

- Ginseng can be used, too. Take a little two weeks on and two weeks off.

- Use Damiana to get pregnant.

- Lecithin and zinc help to open capillaries and produce testosterone.

DNA AND SEX

I believe that everyone has DNA ancestral memories that can have an effect on their life. Even if you think that sex is a wonderful thing, your ancestors may have thought that it was terribly wrong and was only meant for procreation. This may influence how you feel about someone sexually, because of the dual belief system about it. This is why it is important to explore the possibility of the existence of opposing belief systems that can cause friction in your sex life. You may have to do some genetic work on these issues. From a genetic standpoint, we may have inherited all kinds of beliefs from religious and social stigmas about sex. Some of these old concepts may have been viable in the past, but have no place in the present.

So, ask yourself, how do you really feel about relationships on a genetic level? How do you feel about yourself? How do you feel about your birth? How do you feel about your sexuality? What is sexy? Do you feel sex is wrong?

Because the drive for sex is such a powerful force, spiritual traditions have responded to it in various ways throughout history, particularly organized religion, which is based upon creating a way of life for the masses to follow. Obviously, such a powerful force as sex can and has been perceived as something that needs to be controlled. Monogamy and celibacy have thus been widely promoted. In the case of monogamy, it can be said that it was developed to keep the peace, since wanton desires can create longstanding feuds between people. Celibacy was designed in an endeavor to release the attachment to physical and emotional energies through devotion to divinity.

It seems that the attachment to sex is viewed as wicked by some people. With the acts of some misguided individuals, this is perhaps justified, but the whole of the community should not be held accountable for the actions of the few. This has led to an unfortunate blame-game as men relate to women. Some men seem to blame women for their physical desires, desires that perhaps should not be seen as base or carnal, but as a spiritual gift from God, just like anything else that is special in life. If sex were perceived as special, then perhaps even young people would not have such a careless attitude toward it.

Just as important, there is little or no training of our children in relationships with the opposite sex, what to watch for in people, and what to watch out for when we are looking for a soul mate.

Sexuality should be viewed as another feature of leading a spiritual life that teaches us that all aspects of creation, including this embodiment in our physical body, should be considered sacred, particularly when the unity of soul mates becomes true love. In true love, sexual union becomes more that an animalistic act and transcends into something spiritual, into something that is beyond simple materialism. It becomes an alchemical fusion of all the aspects of body, mind, and spirit.

In order to create this alchemical fusion, it is important to work on any negative beliefs that we may have that relate to sex.

THE SEXUAL CHAKRA

When you encounter spiritual people who say that they are not interested in sex or a relationship, it is likely that they have started to shut down their sexual chakra, which is the energy that naturally brings people to them in the first place. Having your sexual chakra open is like having an energy beacon sending out signals to sexually compatible people. If your sexual chakra area is open and you are keeping it open, you are also going to have money, because it opens up your base chakra to attract abundance.

Your sexual chakra has a lot to do with who and what you are – what you feel and what you respect. From the time you are conceived until the time you are born, through all of your life and your relationships with others, the energy of abuse is going to be kept in the sexual chakra area. However, good memories are stored in the sexual chakra as well.

I think that people close down the sexual chakra because of being let down by those they respected as a child. Children have a tendency to pick one or two parental adults to be the 'hero.' When the child feels let down by the 'hero,' it creates distrust and this washes over into relationships later in life.

If your sexual chakra area is open, you will release feelings of abuse and bring in abundance. This is why it is important to keep it open and periodically check to see if it is closed. Doing the ThetaHealing meditation (*page 8*) will balance and open your chakras. (*See also Advanced ThetaHealing.*)

Some of the issues kept in this area are how you feel about sex – if it's bad, if it's good, if it's a sin or not a sin. It also has to do with how you communicate with yourself and others, and with nurturing. If this subject makes you uncomfortable then it is likely that you have some programs that relate to these issues.

One thing that can happen to people who are sensitive to their relationship (and the lack of love therein) is that they have a tendency to open and close their psychic centers, and this can cause physical problems. The trick is to keep these areas open all the time.

When couples marry and have children, a certain percentage of men begin to regard their wife as a mother rather than a sexual partner. By the same token, women shut down their sexual chakra when they don't want to be with their partner or when they sense that their partner doesn't want to be with them. Or, conversely, when they don't want to cheat on their partner.

This causes a lot of physical problems. In women, the adrenals help with testosterone. When the sexual chakra is shut down, I believe that the adrenals can suffer. Another thing that can happen when a couple shuts down their sexual chakras is that they both gain weight and develop intestinal problems. Their estrogen and testosterone levels lower and they have no energy. These hormones give us energy in our daily lives and have other important functions besides sex.

There can even be problems with finances. It is possible to create some abundance from the crown chakra, but this energy is pulled in through the base chakra. If the base chakra is blocked, it isn't likely that the abundance will come in as it should. Remember, abundance isn't only about money. Abundance encompasses many different aspects in life, including relationships and family.

A sexless relationship is a lonely place. However, if the foundation of the union is only based upon sex, then there will be loneliness in a different way. This is what happens to some people – they get married young and find themselves in a relationship with a person who has become the complete opposite of them. They have lost track of each other somewhere along the line.

These are very important aspects of any relationship. Any time that you are sharing DNA with another person, you are helping to create a bond between you. If the sexual energy is lost, then a key aspect will also be lost from the relationship.

People can recognize when someone has a wide-open sexual chakra and healthy hormone levels when they walk into the room. This is why a woman can get so angry when a sexy woman walks by her man! The woman instinctually knows that her territory is being invaded. This happens in seconds and it is all on an instinctual level. The woman just walks by, and instantly the man knows that she is sensual.

PROCREATION

Humans were made to create two sets of families in their lives. You see this with some women. When they are young, they have one set of children, and then when they get older, they have another set of children. Women reach their sexual peak at 35, and this is when some start a second family.

Older Females

From the age of 35 until she is about 45 or 50, a woman is suddenly in another world. Nature has awakened her with a new drive, whispering to her, 'It's time to conceive again.' This is because her body knows that soon she will be past her prime to have children. This is also why 35 to 50-year-old women and 18 to 25-year-old men make good sexual partners – they are both at their sexual peaks. But this doesn't mean that they make good parents … or a good family.

Younger Males

Many women feel that the only thing that men think about is sex. This isn't true, because occasionally they think about other things. But a young man has enormous amounts of testosterone and this makes him think of sex nearly all the time, including when he is in school. If he were in a more primitive setting, he would be mating. The sexual drive in men is unbelievably strong, but if they did not have it, in all honesty they would not want to be around women, so the species would not continue.

Young men have an incredible drive to reproduce and will start investigating their sexuality as soon as they can. They do not see the consequences of their actions, and need to be taught that sex is a sacred and incredibly beautiful thing between people that should not be taken lightly. They should be told that as soon as you share your body with someone, you share DNA with that person.

There is little or no training of our young males about future relationships with the opposite sex. First, nature doesn't activate fully the frontal lobe of males until they are in their mid-twenties. I believe that one of the reasons for this is so that they have the desire to breed without thinking about it. This is one of nature's tricks to make sure we have children in the world and there is propagation of the species. So young men have sex and have babies without thinking it through. It is nature's way of making sure people reproduce.

Older Males

Nature has another trick up its sleeve later in the life of males. At about 45 or 50, men begin to feel a little insecure. We call it the 'midlife crisis.' All of a sudden the man says, 'Do I have everything in my life that I wanted? Have I done everything that I needed to do?'

Suddenly he has a desire to be young again. This is just hormonal and with many men is easily overcome.

It is a fact, though, that men who are with younger women always look younger. Older women with younger men always look younger, too. It's nature's trick to make sure that they do the best that they can in terms of breeding.

FALLING IN LOVE AGAIN

It is possible to fall in love with many different people over the space of a lifetime. Some of us fall in love with our second-grade schoolteacher. Some people fall in love for the first time when they are 16 or 17 years old and they have an idea of what life means to them. When you are 20 years old, you think you know everything, but you are so full of hormones that it is difficult to think straight, and falling in love at this time is generally intense. When you reach 30 years old, you are sure you can make things work in your life, but you still have the capacity to fall in love. When you reach 40, you are just trying to get set for being 50, but there is still hope that love can be found. What does being 50 years old mean to you? Fifty is when you are wise and determined. In some cultures people don't get married until they are 50 years old. Is their love any less? No, the magic of love is still magical.

Science theorizes that we have a gene for falling in love. They think that the 'in love' feeling lasts for one year and this is why in the second year of marriage things are more difficult. I think that this is true with people who fall in love over and over again with different people. They are addicted to the feelings that are released when they meet a new person and they suddenly have a bright and shiny new toy! In a monogamous relationship, you can easily fall in love over and over again with your husband or wife in much the same way. I can't tell you how many times I have fallen in love with Guy.

I think that by the age of 40, we all know what we want in life. We can think clearly, and then all of a sudden what we think is *I'm unhappy and I need to change something*. The challenge is to discern if these thoughts are reproduction driven, or if they are viable issues with our situation. I think that a 'midlife crisis' has a lot to do with looking at your life, but without destroying the family in the process. If you know how to share your feelings, neither of you is going to stray from the other. If you don't know how to share your feelings, then you may stray and end up with the wrong person.

As you get older, your taste in the opposite sex changes, but your interest doesn't go away. I remember when I was a teenager I looked at 50-year-old men in the movies, thinking, *They are so old!* Now, as an adult, I watch the same movies and think, *Charlton Heston – what a handsome man!* Think about Gregory Peck when he got a little older and began to have wrinkles in the corners of his eyes. Now that I am older, I think that this made him even sexier. When Sean Connery was younger, I didn't find him that attractive, but when he got older, man, did he get sexy! Even when he was a 70-year-old man, his voice and his energy made him so appealing. George Clooney and Brad Pitt also seem to just get better the older they get!

I believe that sex is a personal choice and I also believe that there are people in their seventies who are still sexually active. I think that love is much deeper than simple physical contact, and I do visualize that I will be having sex when I am 80.

ONE OR MANY?

When you are a spiritual person and have sex with someone you start to share *spiritual energy* with each other. This bonds your energies in a way that is difficult to define, yet once you have experienced it, you know it is a bond like no other. We all know that the body is still animalistic in some ways. We have desires to breed and we have desires for sex. If you feel no shame about sex and have respect for it, knowing it's a spiritual energy, you may feel differently about it.

This is not the same as thinking that you can love more than one person and have multiple relationships at the same time. I have had people in the metaphysical realm try to tell me that it is the highest form of love when you can love five or six different people, using the excuse of 'God loves everyone.'

I believe that God does love everyone and you probably can love five or six different people. For some people, it's easier to love many people than it is to let someone love you completely. But this doesn't work so well in practical terms, since it is likely that your spirit will be drawn to one of them more than the rest and inevitably someone is going to get jealous and cause friction. I believe that the species is more successful when two people love each other completely. I believe that this is the ultimate spiritual achievement. To me, the supreme bond is to love and be loved completely by one person, and only one person.

I know all about the stance of biologists who say that men have a direct need to mate with more than one woman, but I believe that love prevails over this need. I understand, too, that there are cultures in which one man may have many wives, but I think that this arrangement would be a difficult one for all the parties concerned.

It is not mine to judge, and I believe that a person can definitely love more than one person, but this is dependent upon *the way* you love them. I believe that to say that you love more than one person is a kind of cop-out, because that way you are not obliged to know a person completely, nor are you spiritually committing to them as a partner in order to attain a virtue.

In many instances, people pull *many partners* to them because they are all different aspects of what they want in *one partner*. They are searching for one partner who has all those aspects, one soul mate.

An interesting if perhaps simplistic quote comes from Paul Newman. In an interview he was expressing his love for his wife when somehow the conversation moved to the subject of monogamy. His statement on the subject went something like this: 'Why would I go out for hamburgers when I can go home and have steak?'

The Monogamy Gene

After working with thousands of people, I began to see patterns that suggested the existence of a gene for monogamy as well as a gene for non-monogamy. I believe that approximately 70 per cent of women are born with the monogamy gene and probably 50 per cent of men.

The difference I have observed between people who have it and people who don't is this: if you have no monogamy gene and you meet somebody and have sex with them, you're not going to feel guilty when you go home to your mate. But if you have a monogamy gene, you're going to feel that you've been put through the wringer because of the guilt.

If you've been raised to be monogamous and you don't have the monogamy gene, then you may still feel a little guilty, but not the way you would if you had being instinctively loyal to your partner in your DNA.

Having the monogamy gene doesn't mean that you will be more loyal; loyalty is a spiritual choice. It just means that you will feel guilty when you aren't loyal.

People without the monogamy gene can be loyal, too; they just have to work at it.

Cheating

Once I began to do readings, I found that a fair number of people were cheating in their relationships. This was a strange new realm of human behavior for me and I was interested in their motivations. I found several patterns. Some said they did not receive any love at home. With others, it was a question of self-esteem, while others wanted to 'see if they could,' because of ego. Sometimes they just got into the habit and carried it on throughout their lives.

In this day and age, some people are very afraid of long-term relationships. Sometimes they start an affair with someone who is married so they don't have to commit. This can be an extremely lonely decision for them.

In other instances, there are people in long-term relationships who cheat all the time. These people swear that it helps their relationship because it makes them feel young.

But every cheater I've ever read for has the belief 'I am terrified of letting someone love me.'

There are signs that show that a person who is subtly attempting to have a casual relationship with you is a cheater. When you are looking for a soul mate, you need to be alert for these.

The main one is that they will tell you how unhappy they are in their relationship. If someone starts telling you about their miserable marriage, there is a good chance that they are sending out a signal to see if you have loose moral values. Sometimes they will be blunt and simply come out and ask you.

You may be attracted to them, but know that what a person does in their personal life reflects their true nature. If someone cheats on their spouse, they will cheat in business and in everything else in their life.

Having said that, I've done thousands of readings for good people who are caught in difficult relationships, and anyone can cheat if they are in bad circumstances. For those of you who find yourself in these circumstances, you should know that you are part of God and you deserve to be loved. And you should not settle for being number two in a relationship. I believe that no one should be second best and we all deserve to be loved completely.

A cheat gets to be the 'lover' and never has to be responsible in a relationship. They fall in love again and again with many different people and it becomes an addiction, like smoking one brand of cigarettes and then switching to another brand every few weeks. In a soul-mate relationship, you need to be devoted to your partner as the lover, the husband, the wife, the friend, the nurturer, and so on. This kind of commitment is too much responsibility for some people.

Spiritual Exclusivity

There are also women who have what I call 'goddess energy.' These women always have someone in their bed until they find their true soul mate. Ladies, it is very difficult for a man to fall in love with you when you have been with so many people that you can't remember how many there were. So, if you are promiscuous and you are waiting for a true love, you should consider ending the promiscuity in your life. This will help to hold your soul energy to yourself so that you can find a complete love.

If you really love someone completely, you will never go out of your way to hurt them. So, unless both of you agree to an open relationship, you probably should not engage in this kind of behavior, because it can become addictive.

You may ask, is this realistic for some people? Undoubtedly, some people can't or won't do this. Well, I teach these concepts for people who want to grow spiritually. Promiscuity is not a way for a healer to live and is breaking one of the laws of healing. According to ancient traditions, being focused on one partner builds the soul essence, because a virtue is attained. Spreading your energy out among many people only gives you many soul fragments and part of your energy is lost to others.

If you have been promiscuous, you should pull back your energy from all those different people and come to the realization that you are worth a true and complete love. It is important to know that your body, mind, and soul are all special. It isn't about how many people you've been with, it's about a special person that you can share your life with, without always having to gather your soul fragments (*see page 194*) and expend your energy on those who are undeserving of it. The real way of true divinity is to learn to be loyal and let one person love you completely.

If you want to progress spiritually, it is important to take this step toward allowing someone to know you and to know and love them in return. Knowing that you are first in someone's life is very important for a spiritual relationship. Everyone deserves the chance to advance spiritually in this way.

ThetaHealing is not just a technique that takes us to a theta brainwave to 'make things happen.' It 'makes things happen' by changing our beliefs to make us worthy and clear in our thoughts. This creates 'lite' thoughts that change the planet, and in turn the universe. People who are interested in using the laws of the universe, shifting time, moving matter, and doing amazing things as gods and goddesses need a divine life partner. A person who has many sexual partners at the same time will find it difficult to hold high-vibrational thought forms, move things with the mind, and do amazing healings. With many partners, this scenario just does not work.

LOVE-MAKING

When it comes to being in love, there are no classes that teach you how to be with someone and to be a good lover. What is important is that when you come together in a sexual way, you focus on each other. Many people think that they are supposed to fantasize when they make love. Some men fantasize to make themselves last longer for the woman. But if you refocus on the touch, energy, kindness, and love that you feel for your partner, your love-making will improve. Focusing on the person you are with makes all the difference in the world. Words of kindness can also turn a sexual encounter into love-making.

Sometimes, of course, there is sex, and sometimes there is making love. Neither of these encounters should cause any pain or discomfort. Tell your partner what you want to do and what you don't want to do, or you may become resentful. Make sure you and your partner have the same interests, but above all, if spirituality is your quest, then concentrate on your partner's soul essence and how they make you feel.

Women complain that 'men only want sex.' But isn't sex love? To most men sex is an expression of love, but women complain that men can be superficial when it relates to matters of sex. As you go to the bedroom with your partner, you shouldn't be thinking that it is a chore.

If at the beginning of a relationship the sex is bad or clumsy, this puts a stress on the energy between the budding couple. The first moments of touch that you share are very important between two people who are coming together as soul mates.

Just because you get someone into your bed doesn't mean they will stay there. My father once told me something that I didn't want to admit might be true. He told me that if you were good in bed, you could keep your mate by your side.

Being good in bed isn't about movements or acrobatics. It has a lot to do with the compatibility of your bodies. Much of this comes down to the simple basics of physiology. If the woman is too loose or the man not big enough, or if the man is too big or the woman too tiny, then there are some definite problems at the beginning. A woman should never be too loose for a man. She should be able to tighten up enough for any man. There are exercises that keep a woman tight enough to have numerous orgasms.

A mature male partner will know that he is supposed to please a woman. This means that he should last long enough so that both people have an orgasm. Many men don't realize that they are supposed to satisfy a woman, and this is one reason why they cannot keep a woman.

A sexually satisfied woman is much more emotionally balanced, because she is able to release those pent-up energies. The ancient Taoists believed that they could achieve balanced health by having sex. The also believed that it had to be done in certain ways. They taught 'internal exercises' that kept the sexual energy of both the male and the female working as they should. I refer you to the book I mentioned earlier, *The Complete System of Self-Healing: Internal Exercises* by Stephen Chang.

When you make love to someone you love and really focus on your partner, it is possible to have incredibly spiritual experiences and get closer to the divine.

Seventh-Plane Union

With a compatible soul mate, sexual union can become more that an animalistic act and transcend into something spiritual.

To improve the sexual experience between a couple, I recommend the Taoist deer exercise for both the male and female energies. It can help the woman be more appealing, more sensual, and tighter. It can help the man be more appealing and longer-lasting. It can also put the body into synch and help with sensitivity. If you practice this exercise for a month, it can make both partners hormonally balanced.

Then the couple should go up to the Seventh Plane together while engaging in sex. This make the two people feel as though they have become one energy. The man has to be very focused, clear, and disciplined in this endeavor, so he does not lose track of what he is doing. If the couple is successful, it heightens the sexual experience and they can feel a deep bond between them.

When the souls merge in spiritual union, a pure energy is created between the two people, like a flint striking steel that creates the spark for fire. This fire is ignited in the act of sexual spiritual union. When total intimacy is reached in this union, it is possible to experience colors, lights, and energies that are created from this energy, because you are sharing your whole being, and a bond is created that becomes everlasting.

When two people bond as compatible soul mates, it's supposed to be one of the highest unions in spirituality. To me, this is what sex is supposed to be. In the right sexual union, you should be able to share your whole self with someone – share everything in a merging of two souls. When you find your most compatible soul mate, the union is so deep that you do actually share essences of yourself, even dreams and memories.

This merging of souls doesn't take the fun out of sex. Some people are taught that sex and spirituality are two different things. We learned this from our ancestors. But really, when you merge as true soul mates, the two of you merge in ecstatic energy.

Part III

LIVING WITH A SOUL MATE

Chapter 11

LIVING TOGETHER

Compatible life soul-mate unions are part of the evolution of the Earth. As true partners, a couple should evolve and change together. Part of our development as human beings is to learn to accept others for who and what they are. It is very important that you don't romanticize so much about a partner that you don't see them for who they are. The term 'love is blind' applies to soul mates as well. It is imperative that when you find your soul mate, you accept them for who they are. But you should also bear in mind that you can both become better people through the interaction that can only happen from such a union.

In a sense, we bring out in our companions what we expect. This is why people act differently in different relationships. We are making choices on an unconscious level, giving signals to the person that we are with, bringing out the good in them, or perhaps bringing out the bad.

For instance, I taught Guy how to have a sense of humor, because by the time he came into my life, he was so emotionally traumatized by his prior relationship that he had lost it!

The person you are with should have a matching vibration to your own. If they don't share your vision in life, it can make things difficult. The company you keep is also quite literally important for the health of your heart. You can be affected by the thoughts and actions of the people with whom you are in close proximity.

Really, the only way to survive a relationship with a soul mate is to love yourself. If you don't love yourself, a soul-mate relationship can be very difficult. If you love yourself, then you can recognize that you still love someone else even when you're angry with them. You should never forget that you love your soul mate.

A soul-mate love isn't always an easy love, though. Even if you've known and loved your soul mate in past lives, that doesn't mean they will have exactly the same kind of personality that they did before, and your personality won't be the same either. But generally, whatever their current personality, a soul mate will know exactly how to make us angry, because they know us so well.

One way of gaining an insight into what's going on is through astrology.

ASTROLOGY AND THE SOUL MATE

From the largest galaxy to the smallest particle, everything in the universe has a vibration that connects it with the whole of existence. Because of the interconnectedness of all things, nothing happens by chance and everything in life matters. When you came into this world, you came here for a reason, and the date of your arrival was timed to coincide with certain energies on this Third Plane. The date of your birth is connected to your divine timing, your mission in this life.

With this in mind, when you are asking the Creator deep inner questions, I have a suggestion for you. Ask: 'Where is the best place for me to live, the place that will bring my highest vibration and stimulate my outward and inner energies? Which place has the best energy for me, for my body? Where is the healthiest place for me to live?'

What you should *not* ask is a question like 'Creator, where do you want me to go?' or 'Where do you want me to be?' I will tell you why.

I once had an astrological reading from a professional who charted my horoscope. I don't know if you have ever had one of these, but they are very accurate, informative, and in-depth in their content. Part of the reading focused on where would be the best place for me to live. I was told that according to my horoscope, Spain and Hawaii were the most suited to my energy, and where I lived in Idaho was the very worst place. Apparently, living in Idaho would bring up every internal issue that I had and even draw to me all the initiations that it was possible to have.

The astrologer told me, 'If you can learn to live in Idaho, you can live anywhere. Idaho is an unhealthy place for you to be.'

It became apparent that the Creator knew exactly where to put me to bring up all my issues so that I would find a way to clear them. Had I lived in a place that was easy for me, I would never have created ThetaHealing, which (in part) was born from my environment being hostile to me on every level of my being. Granted, this situation almost killed me a few times, but I did learn to survive. (I finally broke free from it and moved to Montana.)

When the astrologer read Guy's horoscope, he initially told him that I would be a challenge to be with as a soul mate. Since Guy was an Aries with Aries rising and I was a Capricorn with Scorpio rising, I would, in his words, 'chew him up and spit him out.' Initially he couldn't figure out why we were together. However, as the reading progressed, it became clear to him: it seems that Guy has a 'finger of God' in his chart. Apparently this is not a common thing to have in a horoscope and it means that he was born with a specific mission from God. From the astrological reading, it appears that both Guy and I are on a special mission, and that we will carry it out together.

It may be that when you first start dating a person your zodiac sign will fight with their sign. Because Guy is an Aries with Aries rising, he is a homebody. He likes to rule at home. I am a Capricorn, which means my home is my home, so we were headed for a collision of goat against ram!

When we moved in together, Guy was afraid that I would take down all his decorations and replace them with my own. Eventually we put our things together and created a balance of each other's energies and forms of expression. Still, it became very obvious to me that the home was *his*. I had the choice to either fight him for the home or let him have it, and upon reflection, I let him have it.

Now the kitchen is his and he is the king. Because he is the king, he cooks, cleans, and washes the dishes! Since I am the queen, he cooks for me, serves the food to me, and rubs my feet every night, but really he is in charge at home. Whoever decorates, does the laundry, does the dishes, and cleans the house has the power in the house, because they are anchoring their energy into every aspect of it.

The office is mine, and from time to time I have to remind him that this is so. I am in charge at the institute, while the farm, the garden, the labyrinth, and the house are his responsibility.

Some people say that astrology is all hoo-ha, but I have observed that overall, people act like their sun sign and their rising sign. If these are different, they seem to act more like their rising sign. I am a Capricorn with Scorpio rising and I act more like a Scorpio.

When it comes to relationships, look at your moon sign. That shows how your subconscious acts and how you are in a loving relationship.

If you can figure out your soul mate's signs, you will have a good idea how they are going to act in the relationship. Understanding my husband's signs helped me to know how to deal with him.

SETTLING DOWN

When you first get together with your soul mate, the two of you will start a settling down process. In most relationships, the woman will fill the home with her energy and make it the way that she wants it to be. This act goes beyond simple decorating style – it is a direct act of domination in the home. This is all about who will be boss after the courtship phase of the relationship has ended (note that the courtship phase should never have an ending). It is essentially a subconscious power struggle between the partners.

This is something that you want to avoid. It is important to step back and look at the situation from a higher perspective. Even with a divine soul mate, life is all about compromise. As I have said, in my relationship, when we began to have conflict over whose house it was, I stepped back and let Guy have dominance over the house. Capricorns are really home-oriented people and it is hard for them to let go of this kind of control, but I did it for the benefit of the relationship. I had to step back out of the conflict and let Guy love me.

If you are going to make a home with your soul mate, you have to decide who is going to do what in the relationship. Also, you will usually have belief work to do together as you grow and learn from one another.

In my own experience, it is best to share the energy of the house decoration with your partner. If the woman takes over too much, the man can begin to feel insignificant in his home. If the man is dominant, the woman will begin to feel powerless and devoid of expression. In same-sex relationships, who is dominant depends on the personality of the people involved, but the same dynamic is at work.

Always blend the décor so that it meets both of your needs. If there is no compromise in this aspect of a relationship, this can cause all kinds of resentments that fester in the unconscious mind and manifest into reality with outbursts of anger.

This is why I feel that it is best if new couples do not live in a house that was previously owned by one of them. It is best to move into a new house that gives the couple a fresh start without the burden of the beliefs that are likely to be inherent in the house.

Downloading Happiness into the Home

When you make a home together as a couple, be sure to download the right kind of feelings into your house to create harmony in the relationship.

I believe that whenever we touch a solid inanimate object we leave a magnetic memory imprint within it. This explains how what we call inanimate objects can be programmed with certain attributes. We can use this to charge our environment for our benefit.

If you charge the items in your house with a purpose, they will only emanate the energy of that purpose. They will reflect it back to you, giving you a safe haven in which to recharge your mind, so you can nurture the relationship. For example:

- Your kitchen table should be programmed that there is always an abundance of food, and that whoever eats at that table leaves full and satisfied.

- Your walls should allow you to feel safe.

- Your couch should be charged to feel comfortable and inviting.

- Statues and rocks can reflect sacredness and project abundance. All minerals hold memory. One thing you can do with a crystal is to download Seventh-Plane energy into it, then place it in a room. It will emit the Seventh-Plane energy into the house.

- The bed should be programmed with comfort, love, rest, and playfulness.

- Pictures can be charged with nurturing, honor, and inspiration (depending on the theme).

- Carvings can be charged with the appreciation of beauty, majesty, and power.

Program all the objects in your home and space with your desired intentions.

PROGRAM AN INANIMATE OBJECT

1. Center yourself in your heart and visualize going down into Mother Earth, which is a part of All That Is.

2. Go up through your crown chakra in a ball of light and project your consciousness out past the stars to the universe.

3. Go beyond the universe, past the layers of light, through the golden light, past the jelly-like substance that is the Laws, into a pearly, iridescent white light, the Seventh Plane of Existence.

4. Make the command and request:

> 'Creator of All That Is, it is commanded that this article be programmed with the ability of [name ability]. Thank you! It is done, it is done, it is done.'

5. Witness the download going from the Creator into the article.

6. As soon as the process is finished, rinse yourself off in Seventh-Plane energy and stay connected to it.

PROGRAM YOUR ENVIRONMENT
TO ENHANCE YOUR LIFE

1. Go up to the Seventh Plane as before.

2. Make the command:

> 'Creator of All That Is, it is commanded that
> everything in my environment enhances my life.
> Thank you! It is done, it is done, it is done.'

3. Witness the articles in your house and surroundings being downloaded with energies that enrich your life.

4. As soon as the process is finished, rinse yourself off in Seventh-Plane energy and stay connected to it.

HUMAN INTERACTION AND THE NEW FAMILY

Women who have children offer something extra in a relationship: you get the woman and the children in the deal. When you marry these women, you are marrying the whole family. This sometimes is an unfortunate truth. The other truth is that a large percentage of families (both rich and poor) can be a *Jerry Springer Show*. This is a consideration when you marry someone. How can you get along?

Little girls seem to like the boyfriends/new husbands and little boys like the girlfriends/new wives. This situation can be reversed, of course. However, a man who has a new partner with children will generally find a girl will adapt better, while a boy will be fighting for his place as the man of the house. These challenges are real. Whatever situation you are faced with, though, shopping is a good thing to do with the little girls!

It is important to remember that we humans act instinctually in our relationships with others. For instance, men do not become as easily attached to another person's children as women do. There is a better chance that a woman will accept another woman's children as her own. This is because as the female of the species and by her nature and instinct, a woman is a nurturer. We have to remember that no matter how civilized we have become, we are still in an animal kingdom of our own.

A good example of this is observed when a man meets a woman who has a tiny baby. That baby will instinctually begin to put out different pheromones, which are designed to make the man fall in love with it.

Adopted babies will even change their features to match the parents in an instinctual effort at acceptance. A good example is this story about my friend who is a doctor; he is the gynecologist who delivered my granddaughter. Over the years he has delivered thousands of babies, and he kisses each on the forehead after it is born (though his mask). He once delivered a little boy and displayed the child to the mother, but she said, 'Take it away from me. I never want to see it again.' My friend called his wife and asked her if they could adopt the little boy. She agreed. As time went on, the boy looked more like the doctor than his biological children did.

This is the kind of human interaction that causes a mother to instinctually want to care for a baby. A good example of this kind of behavior in women was when my daughters had their children. I allowed them to take care of them at work, and all the other women in the office took on the responsibility of caring for the babies, too. And the energy between the women in the office became much smoother.

To take a different scenario, when a divorce happens, the parent who is left at home and the children will adapt to the changes in their environment and swap roles. If the father leaves, the mother will adapt and become the wage-earner and take on the role of the father, and one of the older children will take on the role of the mother.

It can be very difficult for the children once the parents begin to find other partners after the divorce. A child will fill a void in the family as needed, so, for instance, when a single mother meets a new man, her son will naturally become antagonistic toward him since the man is interfering in his territory. This can be a challenge for the mother and is the root of much conflict between stepfathers and young boys. A stepfather will generally accept girls more easily than boys, since the males will be in competition.

What I find to be a challenge is when mothers refuse to share their children with the stepfather. In many instances they don't want to share the love that the child has for them with anyone else. In this situation, if the beliefs of the mother are changed so that she can share the child's love with the stepfather, then the family dynamics can change. Belief work should be the first thing that you do when bringing another partner into the mix.

If a stepfather has children from a past relationship, he may favor his own children over those of the new relationship, whereas a stepmother will often accept all the children. I believe that the mothers who do not accept children don't have the pheromone receptors that other women do.

Whatever the dynamics of a new family, they can be changed by using downloads:

- For the man: 'I can accept another person's child as my own.'

- For the mother: 'I know how to share my children with another person.'

- For the child: 'I know how to accept this person as an extra parent.'

Chapter 12

RECOVERING RELATIONSHIPS ... OR MOVING ON

When a couple first marries, passion and romance are present in the relationship, but over time the pair may forget to make each other feel special, and women in particular want these things to happen spontaneously. I have seen many men who have forgotten to keep the romance going, but marriage is a two-way street, and often women don't realize that men don't work this way and need to be told that they need to be romantic.

So often I have seen a woman who felt that her husband was her soul mate when they were first married, but over time starts feeling that something is missing in the relationship. She wants a knight in shining armor to sweep her off her feet in a purple mist of romance and passion! Everything else in the relationship might be working fine and it might have taken years for the man to become what she wants, but now she wants to get rid of him. Then, after they have been divorced for a while, she realizes that she misses him terribly.

Her knight does not materialize; she comes to the realization that her ex-husband was her soul mate.

Many people get divorced or leave a long-term relationship before they should. It is only when they break up or get a divorce that they remember how much they love the other person, and by then that person has likely moved on.

Recovering a relationship is worth the time, because long-term relationships, marriage and family are all important, as are the feelings and energy that two people create between them.

However, you cannot recover these feelings alone. If one of you wants to keep the relationship going and the other person doesn't, it makes recovery very difficult.

CREATING LISTS

By the time that a relationship needs repair, we have created lists in our mind of things that we don't like about the other person.

So the first thing that I suggest as an exercise is to write down everything that you like and love about the person you are in a relationship with. This will help to remind you of all the reasons why you fell in love in the first place. It will take you back to the beginning when your love was fresh and new.

Once you have been reminded of all these positive feelings, I suggest that you magnify them a little bit and then perhaps you can retrieve the love that you have lost.

Belief work is the next step that I suggest for couples in a difficult relationship. When the soul-mate class first came out, it repaired many marriages and relationships because it gave couples a way to repair their feelings through belief work.

BREAKING UP

Not every soul-mate relationship works out, though. Due to many factors, one of the partners can cease to love the other person. When this happens, they no longer want to be with them and things cannot be recovered.

Life is about choices. If you wish to break up from your present relationship, this is between you and God. Ask God if your relationship could (or should) be saved and how.

Keeping open lines of communication with the person is all important. You might be with your compatible soul mate and not know it. This may be because you do not communicate with them.

But if you find that this relationship cannot be saved, it is at this point that you should decide to ask for a new soul mate.

Also, when you are breaking up with someone, it is best to abstain from sex with them for at least three to four weeks so that you don't have such a deep connection with each other.

The sexual connection is one reason why people have such a difficult time breaking up. When we become romantically involved with someone, our spiritual energy becomes integrated with that person to a certain extent. As we have seen, when we have sex with them, we exchange DNA both of a physical and spiritual nature, and this lasts for at least seven years. This spiritual DNA is one of the reasons why many of us find it difficult to break away from a person even though we have irreconcilable differences with them. We need to take back the soul fragments we gave them, but the body can only accept so many at a time, so these soul fragments can only come back to us in layers.

Retrieving Soul Fragments from Past Relationships

This exercise will do incredible things for your spiritual strength. Do you still think about a past love from 10 years ago? You may still carry a soul fragment from that person. To release and replace soul fragments from a particular person, make the command that all soul fragments that have been exchanged between you be rinsed, cleansed, and returned to both parties.

If you are currently in a happy relationship with someone and intend to stay together, it isn't necessary to call back the soul fragments that the two of you have exchanged.

If you decide to have soul fragments returned to you from a past lover or spouse, don't be surprised if they call you up out of the blue in an attempt to re-establish a connection with you. Many of the people who took our first soul-mate class re-established their connection with their childhood sweethearts and got married to them.

Here are two processes for retrieving soul fragments in general. One is for doing the process on another person; the other is for doing the process on yourself.

1. Center yourself in your heart and visualize going down into Mother Earth, which is a part of All That Is.

2. Go up through your crown chakra in a ball of light and project your consciousness out past the stars to the universe.

3. Go beyond the universe, past the layers of light, through the golden light, past the jelly-like substance that is the Laws, into a pearly, iridescent white light, the Seventh Plane of Existence.

4. Make the command and request:

    > *For someone else:* 'Creator of All That Is,
    > it is commanded that all soul fragments from all
    > generations of time, eternity, and between
    > time from [individual's name] be released,
    > cleansed, and returned to them. Thank
    > you! It is done, it is done, it is done.'

    > *For yourself:* 'Creator of All That Is, it is commanded
    > that all my soul fragments from all generations
    > of time, eternity, and between time be released,
    > cleansed, and returned to me, [name yourself].
    > Thank you! It is done. It is done. It is done.'

5. Witness the fragments being returned.

6. As soon as the process is finished, rinse yourself off with Seventh-Plane energy and stay connected to it.

DIVORCE

I am personally very grateful for the institution of divorce because it enabled me to leave relationships that were obviously not going to work. I had been divorced three times before I met Guy.

I have to admit, I was somewhat naïve about relationships when I was younger. I found that the first two men I married were incompatible with me and the third was very peculiar! I should have dated these men for a much longer time before I married them and had I done so it is likely that I would have seen that we were not compatible.

In the USA, many couples get divorced, mostly because they realize that they are with the wrong partner. But sometimes people get divorced from the right partner because they don't want to go through hardships to get to a point where they get along. Many people realize that their ex-husband or ex-wife was actually their soul mate after they have broken up with them, because they were looking for their soul mate instead of working on their relationship. This has been the case with many women I've observed over the years. In a way, a divorce is good for those who are incompatible and bad for those who have jumped ship too soon.

If a situation cannot be recovered, though, divorce is inevitable. If there are children from the relationship, it is important to make this transition as smooth as possible for them. Divorce can become so nasty that the parents talk badly about each other in front of the children. This situation should be avoided. The children also deserve to see both parents after the break-up.

ENERGETIC DIVORCE

How to release a commitment that is not serving you:

1. Center yourself in your heart and visualize going down into Mother Earth, which is a part of All That Is.

2. Go up through your crown chakra in a ball of light and project your consciousness out past the stars to the universe.

3. Go beyond the universe, past the layers of light, through the golden light, past the jelly-like substance that is the Laws, into a pearly, iridescent white light, the Seventh Plane of Existence.

4. Make the command and request:

   'Creator of All That Is, it is commanded that [person's name] and I are released from the commitment of this marriage that is past, in the highest and best way, so that I might meet my soul mate. I have the correct definition of all the people in my life and of God. Thank you! It is done, it is done, it is done.'

5. Witness the energy of the bond being sent to the Creator's light.

6. As soon as the process is finished, rinse yourself off with Seventh-Plane energy and stay connected to it.

Please understand that none of what I have discussed with you is set in stone. You can change your reality so it is possible to make a soul mate out of the person that you are currently with. This information is not a license to break up your current relationship. You may be with your soul mate and not even know it!

Whatever your situation, here is my soul-mate prayer:

Creator of All That Is,
All that I can and will be, today, upon my request, I give as a
  prayer to thee.
I pray that I will find my person, the one who is for me.
The one who can join with me,
And allow me to be free.

I pray that this person will be the one and only one.
The one who makes my heart feel grand,
To become as one with me.

I pray to you hear my plea and I will find the one for me.

Over the waters and over the sea, I know there is the one for me.
I pray that I will find them soon,
And they will find me.
Then we will live our lives
Together as one.

With the knowing that being with another may not easy,
With the knowing that being with another can be a challenge,
This is just the thing that fills me with glee.
I pray that I will find the one to share my life,
To watch the sunsets and laugh and play with me.

To grow together until we are very old,
Until the time to leave has come,
I pray that we will leave together for a higher plane.
This true love, I do deserve,
With this request, I now pray, that I will soon be served.

It is my hope that I have helped you on your journey to a compatible soul mate. Good luck!

RESOURCES

ThetaHealing® is an energy-healing modality founded by Vianna Stibal, based in Bigfork, Montana, with certified instructors around the world. The classes and books of ThetaHealing® are designed as a therapeutic self-help guide to develop the ability of the mind to heal. ThetaHealing® offers seminars (*see page 202*) the following books:

ThetaHealing® (Hay House, 2006, 2010)

Advanced ThetaHealing® (Hay House, 2011)

ThetaHealing® Diseases and Disorders (Hay House, 2011)

On the Wings of Prayer (Hay House, 2012)

ThetaHealing® Rhythm for Finding Your Perfect Weight (Hay House, 2013)

Seven Planes of Existence (Hay House, 2016)

For further information about schedules for ThetaHealing®
seminars, see: www.thetahealing.com. Alternatively, you can join us
on social media:

 ThetaHealingbyVianna

 ThetaHealingbyVianna

 @thethetahealing

 thethetahealing

 ThetaHealingVianna

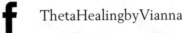 www.thetahealing.com
www.thetahealinginstituteofknowledge.com

ABOUT THE AUTHOR

Vianna Stibal is a young grandmother, an artist and a writer. Her natural charisma and compassion for those in need of help have also led to her being known as a healer, intuitive, and teacher.

After being taught how to connect with the Creator to co-create and facilitate the unique process called ThetaHealing®, Vianna knew that she must share this gift with the world. It was this love and appreciation for the Creator and humanity that allowed her to develop the ability to see clearly into the human body and witness many instant healings.

Her encyclopedic knowledge of the body's systems and deep understanding of the human psyche, based on her own experience as well as the insight given to her by the Creator, make Vianna the perfect practitioner of this amazing technique. She has successfully worked with such medical challenges as hepatitis C, Epstein-Barr virus, AIDS, herpes, various types of cancers, and many other disorders, diseases, and genetic defects.

Vianna knows that the ThetaHealing® technique is teachable, but beyond that she knows that it needs to be taught. She conducts seminars all over the world to teach people of all races, beliefs and religions. She has trained teachers and practitioners who are working in 14 countries, but her work will not stop there! She is committed to spreading this healing paradigm throughout the world.

Guy Stibal is a former rancher, historian, writer, romantic, and follower of the bright knowledge in all things. He has been the spiritual inspiration for Vianna since 1998 when they found one another and went on the wings of prayer to create ThetaHealing®.

www.thetahealing.com

NOTES

NOTES

We hope you enjoyed this Hay House book. If you'd like to receive our online catalog featuring additional information on Hay House books and products, or if you'd like to find out more about the Hay Foundation, please contact:

Hay House, Inc., P.O. Box 5100, Carlsbad, CA 92018-5100
(760) 431-7695 or (800) 654-5126
(760) 431-6948 (fax) or (800) 650-5115 (fax)
www.hayhouse.com® • www.hayfoundation.org

———

Published in Australia by: Hay House Australia Pty. Ltd.,
18/36 Ralph St., Alexandria NSW 2015
Phone: 612-9669-4299 • *Fax:* 612-9669-4144
www.hayhouse.com.au

Published in the United Kingdom by: Hay House UK, Ltd.,
The Sixth Floor, Watson House, 54 Baker Street, London W1U 7BU
Phone: +44 (0)20 3927 7290 • *Fax:* +44 (0)20 3927 7291
www.hayhouse.co.uk

Published in India by: Hay House Publishers India,
Muskaan Complex, Plot No. 3, B-2, Vasant Kunj, New Delhi 110 070
Phone: 91-11-4176-1620 • *Fax:* 91-11-4176-1630
www.hayhouse.co.in

———

<u>Access New Knowledge.</u>
<u>Anytime. Anywhere.</u>

Learn and evolve at your own pace
with the world's leading experts.

www.hayhouseU.com

Printed in the United States
by Baker & Taylor Publisher Services